The

CAT'S MEOW

Purr-fect Quilts for
Cat Lovers

JANET KIME

CREDITS

Editor-in-Chief . . . . Barbara Weiland
Technical Editor . . . . Ursula Reikes
Managing Editor . . . . Greg Sharp
Copy Editor . . . . Liz McGehee
Proofreader . . . . Tina Cook
Text & Cover Design . . . . Karin LaFramboise
Typesetting . . . . Karin LaFramboise
Photography . . . . Brent Kane
Illustration and Graphics . . . Brian Metz
Janet Kime

Printed in the United States of America
99 98 97 96 95   6 5 4 3

Mission Statement

We are dedicated to providing quality products that encourage creativity and promote self-esteem in our customers and our employees.

We strive to make a difference in the lives we touch.

That Patchwork Place is an employee-owned, financially secure company.

ACKNOWLEDGMENTS

I am indebted to Joel T. Patz for several design ideas, including the one little imp in Firehouse Dogs. Iris Westwood's Bow Tie Buddy pattern was the inspiration for Kelvie's Kitties and Fish Dreams. As always, the patience and good will of my friends at Needle and I and in my island sewing/support group were invaluable.

I owe special thanks to Virginia Morrison. No crisis was too alarming, no deadline too imminent for my own personal elf.

DEDICATION

For Susan and Sarah

Library of Congress Cataloging-in-Publication Data

Kime, Janet
    The cat's meow / Janet Kime.
      p.   cm.
    ISBN 1-56477-061-3 :
    1. Patchwork—Patterns. 2. Cats in art I. Title.
TT835.K4953 1994
746.9'7—dc20   94-13380
                        CIP

Contents

INTRODUCTION

Quilters love cats. I'm not sure why we quilters are so drawn to our fluffy companions. Perhaps it is because we admire graceful design, subtle colors, and the feel of natural fibers. The attraction definitely travels both ways; we love our cats and they love our quilts.

It was especially fun for me to design the quilts in this book, since they combine my favorite hobby and some of my favorite friends. As I sketched and cut and sewed, I thought of the cats I've known over the years. Mickie, watching me rotary cut, perched on the far corner of my cutting board with his tail wrapped around his feet. Pookah, more pack rat than kitten, loping determinedly through the living room with an oven mitt bigger than she is. Tansy, shinnying along a tree branch, upside down like a tree sloth. Tiny Lissa, flattened down in the pasture grass, stalking a goat. And the newest kitten, Molly, dancing across my keyboard and deleting the third chapter of this book.

I've tried to capture here some of the essential characteristics of cats: their grace and calm, their cuddlesome nature, their whimsy. For every quilter who has ever loved a cat, this book is for you.

GENERAL DIRECTIONS

PREPARING FABRIC

Use 100% cotton fabrics for your quilts. Blends are more difficult to work with; they are slippery, they are often not tightly woven and warp out of shape, and they don't press with a sharp crease. On the plus side, blends are more durable, often less expensive, and are almost always more lightfast. But most quilters prefer the softness and easy handling of natural fibers. They protect their quilts from strong light, and when they do fade, they call it mellowing.

I prewash all my fabrics, putting them through regular cycles of the washing machine and dryer. I do this mainly because I plan to machine wash and dry most of my quilts and don't want any surprises after the quilt is constructed. I also prefer to remove the finish that is applied to most fabrics. This is a matter of personal preference. If you would rather keep the crisp finish (it will disappear the first time you wash the quilt), be sure to test your fabrics for colorfastness. One good method is to baste a small piece of your fabric to a small piece of white fabric and set it aside in a shallow dish of warm water for an hour or so. If your fabric doesn't bleed onto the white fabric, it shouldn't bleed when you wash the quilt.

If you don't prewash your fabric, do steam-press it to preshrink it. If a fabric has a linear design that has become skewed, try to even up the design as you steam-press the fabric.

ROTARY CUTTING

You can prepare simple shapes for piecing much faster and more accurately by rotary cutting than by drawing around templates. Cutting dimensions for all squares and rectangles are provided; piecing templates are provided only for the odd-shaped pieces in Kelvie's Kitties and Fish Dreams. Several of the designs are simple enough to be your first rotary-cutting project.

You will need at least three pieces of equipment: a rotary cutter, a cutting mat designed for rotary cutters, and one or two transparent acrylic rulers. Don't try to rotary cut without the special mat; you will quickly ruin the cutting blade. Ideally, you should have a mat that is 24" in at least one dimension and a 6" x 24" ruler. A second ruler is not absolutely necessary if your mat has a 1" grid drawn on it, but a 12" ruler and/or a 6" Bias Square® is handy.

1. Press your fabric before cutting. Fold it with selvages together and lay it on the cutting mat with the fold toward you.
2. If you don't have a second ruler, place the folded edge on one of the grid lines on the mat, then line up your long ruler with a vertical grid line so that the ruler just covers the raw edges of the fabric.

   If you have a second ruler, place it close to the left edge of the fabric and align the edge of the ruler with the fold. Lay the long ruler next to the short ruler so that it just covers the raw edges of the fabric, then remove the short ruler. Now cut the fabric with the rotary cutter, rolling the blade away from you, along the side of the long ruler.

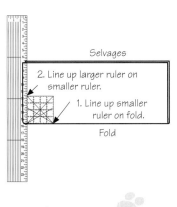

Selvages

2. Line up larger ruler on smaller ruler.

1. Line up smaller ruler on fold.

Fold

TIP

This first cut is called a clean-up cut. It tidies the edge of your fabric and ensures that the next cut will be exactly perpendicular to the fold. If the cuts are not perpendicular to the fold, when you open the strip, it will have a dogleg instead of being perfectly straight. Recheck the angle of your ruler after every two or three cuts and make another clean-up cut whenever necessary.

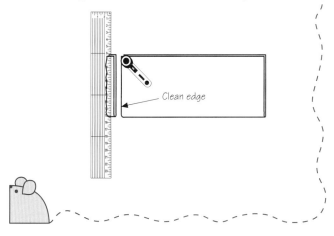

Clean edge

3. After you have tidied the edge of the fabric, you are ready to cut the pieces for your quilt. Align the required measurement on the ruler with the newly cut edge of the fabric. Cut strips across the width of the fabric, from selvage to selvage, in the required width.

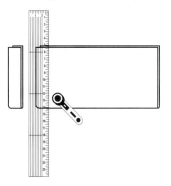

To cut squares:

Cut strips in the required widths. Trim away the selvage ends of the strip and crosscut into pieces of the desired size. For example, if your design calls for 6 squares, each 4" x 4", cut a 4"

strip across the width of the fabric, trim off the selvages, then make 3 crosscuts, each 4" wide.

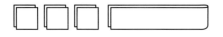

To cut half-square triangles:

Cut a square once diagonally. The short sides of a half-square triangle are on the straight grain of the fabric. Cut the square ⅞" larger than the finished short side of the required triangle to allow for seam allowances.

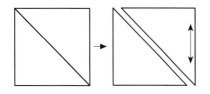

To cut quarter-square triangles:

Cut a square twice diagonally. The long side of a quarter-square triangle is on the straight grain of the fabric. Cut a square 1¼" larger than the finished long side of the required triangle to allow for seam allowances.

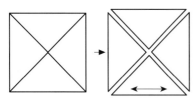

MACHINE PIECING

Maintaining an accurate ¼"-wide seam allowance is extremely important when machine piecing. If seams are not accurate, the seam lines of the designs won't match up, the points of your triangles won't be pointed, the blocks won't fit together properly, and the whole piece won't lie flat.

For example, suppose that you have 8" blocks and a pieced border of 1" squares. Eight of the border squares should equal the width of one block. If your seams are only 1/16" too wide, however, too much fabric is taken up in the seam allowances, and eight of the squares sewn side to side will be ½" too short. (8 x 1/16" = ½") If your quilt is eight blocks wide, your strip of sixty-four border squares will be 4" too short! (64 x 1/16" = 4")

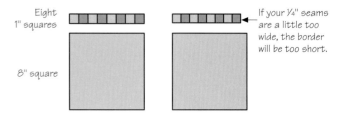

Eight 1" squares

8" square

If your ¼" seams are a little too wide, the border will be too short.

On many sewing machines, the edge of the presser foot is exactly ¼" from the needle. On some machines, the needle position is movable. On other machines, you will need to make a ¼" seam guide by placing a piece of masking tape on the throat plate.

1. Check your machine with a piece of ¼" graph paper. Cut along one of the grid lines.
2. Slip the paper under the presser foot and lower the needle onto the line ¼" from the cut edge. Is the cut edge exactly at the edge of the presser foot? If it isn't, place a piece of masking tape along the cut edge of the paper. This is your ¼" seam guide.
3. Test the accuracy of your ¼" seam guide by sewing a pieced block and measuring it. Even if you appear to be making accurate ¼" seams, your block may be too small. This happens because a little of the fabric is taken up by the bump where each seam allowance is pressed. Most quilters find they need to take a seam allowance that is just a thread or two under ¼". Practice making slight alterations in your seam width until your blocks are consistently the right size. Being fussy at this stage is time well spent.

PRESSING

Careful and thorough pressing is one of the most important, and often most neglected, aspects of quiltmaking. Some quilters set up a small portable ironing board next to the sewing machine. I like to get up and walk around, but I plan ahead so I can sew in batches of ten, twenty, or thirty identical seams and then take the pieces to the ironing board.

There are two basic rules of pressing when you machine sew.

1. Press all seam allowances to one side. They are pressed to one side for strength.

Pressing the seam allowances to one side also allows you to press matching seams in opposite directions; you can then butt seams against each another and more easily match seam lines. In this book, arrows tell you which direction to press seam allowances, so that when you have to match seam lines several steps later, the seam allowances will already be pressed in opposite directions.

When it isn't necessary to match seams, the pressing directions indicate the direction that will reduce bulk. Occasionally, seams are pressed open to reduce bulk when several seams come together at one point. When seam allowances are pressed open, however, the stitching of the seam is exposed and more subject to wear. When bulk is not an issue, press toward the darker fabric.

2. Press each seam before crossing it with another seam. This is the rule quiltmakers tend to ignore, usually with unfortunate results. If you don't press a seam flat before you cross it with another seam, a little tuck will form where the seam allowance is folded to one side. Once you cross that tuck with another seam, the tuck is caught in the stitching and becomes permanent; no amount of pressing will flatten it out. These little tucks will make your block smaller than it should be.

Discipline yourself to press your seams before proceeding to the next step. From the front of the piece, push the broad side of the iron sideways into the bump of the seam and flatten it out.

SPEED PIECING

Speed piecing is a combination of rotary cutting and shortcut sewing techniques.

Strip Units

Many speed-pieced designs require a strip unit, which is made by sewing fabric strips together lengthwise. The strip unit is pressed and then crosscut into segments. The segments are then sewn together to make a design.

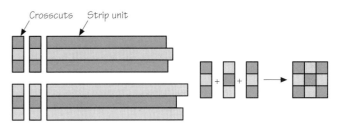

Crosscuts   Strip unit

1. Sew the strips together carefully, with exact ¼"-wide seams, so all the finished strip widths are equal. The unit must also be straight; if the bottom fabric feeds into the sewing machine faster than the top fabric, or vice versa, the unit will curve. To combat this tendency, sew pairs of strips together from top to bottom; then sew the pairs to each other from bottom to top.

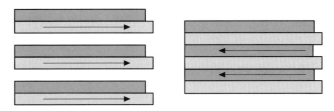

Arrows indicate stitching direction

2. Press the strip unit carefully so that it lies perfectly flat, with no pleats at the seams. The pattern instructions will tell you which direction to press the seam allowances. Press from the back first.

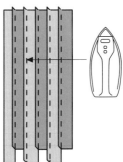

Flip the unit over and press thoroughly from the front, pushing the broad side of the iron into the bump at each seam and flattening it out. If the unit curves just slightly, you may be able to steam it back into line. If not, make frequent clean-up cuts as you cut segments. The segments must be perpendicular to the seam lines, or your little squares will not be square.

Speed-Pieced Ears

Many of the cats in this book have speed-pieced ears. The ear section looks like an odd-shaped piece of background fabric with a triangle of cat fabric at each end. Instead of using templates for these pieces and dealing with several stretchy bias edges, you can make the ear section from a rectangle of background fabric and two squares of cat fabric.

1. With a ruler, draw a diagonal line on the wrong side of the two cat fabric squares. Sew them to the ends of the background rectangle as shown, stitching on the diagonal line.

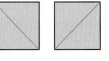

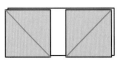

2. Trim away the corners, leaving about ¼" for seam allowances; then press the seam allowances toward the cat fabric.

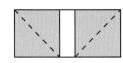

3. If the cat fabric has a stripe or directional print, you will probably want the ears to match the rest of the cat. Position the ear square so the pattern is perpendicular to the pattern in the rest of the cat. If the pattern has an up-and-down design as well, place the up end at the edge of the background rectangle, not toward the center.

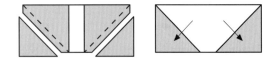

4. The unit may distort into a curve as you press it open. If this happens, pull it back into

shape by grasping the ends of the stitched diagonal line and pulling gently.

If piece is curved, pull along direction of arrows.

TIP

Whenever there is a choice, start stitching the diagonal along an edge of the fabric. It is easier than starting at a point.

Start stitching here.

If you must start at a point, lower the needle ¼" in from the point, carefully backstitch a few stitches, then stitch forward.

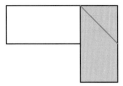

Speed-Pieced Bodies

Speed piecing can also be used to connect two long pieces that are joined on a diagonal. Instead of using templates to cut two odd-shaped pieces, cut two rectangles.

1. Lay one on top of the other at right angles and draw a diagonal line with a ruler as shown. Before you sew, pin along the stitching line, or hold it in place and open up the unit to make sure you drew the diagonal in the correct direction.

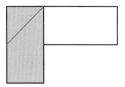

2. Sew on the drawn line. Trim away the excess fabric, leaving about ¼" for a seam allow-

ance. The seam allowance can be pressed in either direction.

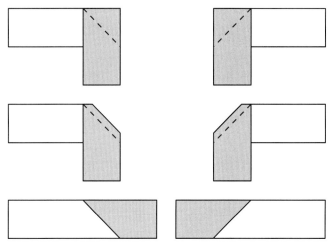

Half-Square Triangle Units

The triangle square is a common unit in pieced designs. It is traditionally made by piecing two half-square triangles together to make a square. There are a number of techniques for speed-piecing half-square triangle units. Any book on rotary-cut quilts, such as *Rotary Riot* or *Shortcuts To the Top,* will include at least one method.

Use the following simple technique for speed piecing half-square triangle units.

1. Cut two squares the same size and draw a diagonal line on the wrong side of one of the squares.
2. Place the squares right sides together; sew a scant ¼" away on both sides of the drawn diagonal.
3. Cut on the diagonal line. You have two half-square triangle units. Press seam allowances toward the darker fabric.

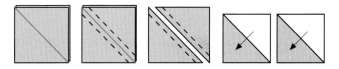

PAPER-PATCH APPLIQUÉ

I prefer and recommend the appliqué method called paper patch. Each piece takes a little

time to prepare, but even beginners can quickly achieve smooth curves and precise shapes.

The appliqué templates do not include seam allowances. Occasionally, when the edge of the piece will lie on the outer edge of the block, the seam allowance is included on one or two sides. When this is the case, the seam allowance is clearly indicated. Edges that will be covered by another piece are indicated with a dotted line and do not need to be turned under.

1. Trace the template on plastic template material and cut out exactly on the drawn line. Then trace around the template on a piece of lightweight card stock or construction paper. Cut the paper piece out carefully, making any curves as smooth as possible. Refer to the illustration of the quilt and label the right side of each paper piece.
2. Lay the paper piece right side down on the wrong side of your fabric. Pin it in place. Cut out the fabric, adding a ¼-wide seam allowance all around the paper piece.
3. Fold the seam allowance under and baste it in place, sewing through the paper piece. Pull the seam allowance as smoothly as possible over curves. When you have basted all around, the fabric should be quite taut over the paper piece.

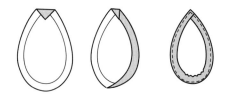

Clip around inside curves almost to the paper piece. Make the clips at least ¼" apart or the fabric will fray. When you come to a corner, baste one edge down all the way to the corner, then fold the other edge over it and continue basting.

4. After you have basted the paper patch, press it thoroughly. Leave the paper and the basting stitches in. Appliqué the piece to the background fabric with an almost invisible stitch. Use thread that matches the appliqué piece, not the background fabric. Catch just a few threads at the edge of the piece. Only a tiny stitch should show on the front of

the quilt; all the "traveling" is done on the wrong side.

Appliqué stitch

5. Stitch almost all the way around the paper patch, leaving 1"–2" unstitched. Remove the basting threads, then reach in and pull out the paper. If the paper tears, use a pair of tweezers to pull out any fragments or make a small slit in the background fabric and pull out any hard-to-reach pieces. It isn't necessary to sew up the slit; the stitching all around the paper patch will stabilize the area. After you have removed all the paper, finish appliquéing the piece.

ASSEMBLING THE BLOCKS

Sewing quilt blocks together into a quilt top is called setting the quilt. The blocks can be arranged either in a straight set or a diagonal set.

For a straight set, sew the blocks together into rows, then sew the rows together.

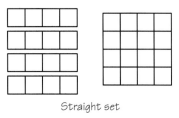
Straight set

For a diagonal set, set the blocks on point and sew them together into diagonal rows. Add triangles to the end of each row to square up the quilt.

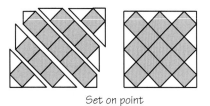
Set on point

Sashing

Sashing strips are strips of fabric sewn between the blocks. The strips isolate the blocks, making the individual design of each block easier to see. Sashing strips are added as the blocks are sewn together. Short strips are sewn between the blocks in each row, then long strips are sewn between the rows as they are sewn together. Some quilts have cornerstones, which are little squares where the sashing strips intersect. Cornerstones can be plain squares, pieced, or even appliquéd.

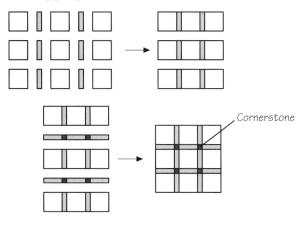
Cornerstone

ADDING BORDERS

The border frames the quilt design and contains it. A border can be made from plain fabric strips, or it can have elaborate pieced or appliquéd designs.

Straight-Cut Borders

For a simple straight-cut border, add border strips to the sides of the quilt and press, then add strips to the top and bottom.

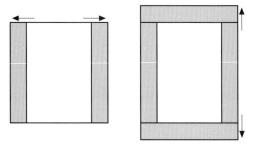
Straight-Cut Border

Although exact measurements are provided for straight-cut borders, measure your quilt first and cut the border strips to fit. Measure the

width and the length in two or three places toward the center of the quilt rather than along the edges.

Mitered Borders

For a mitered border, cut each border strip the length of that side of the quilt, plus three times the width of the border. This allows enough fabric at each end for the miter, plus a little extra for safety.

1. Sew on all four border strips before you make the miters. Start and stop ¼" in from the corners and backstitch for strength. Do not press the seam allowances yet.

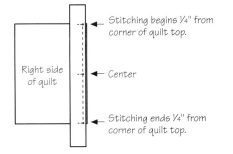

Stitching begins ¼" from corner of quilt top.

Right side of quilt

Center

Stitching ends ¼" from corner of quilt top.

2. To mark the miter, lay a corner of the quilt out flat, wrong side up. Straighten the long ends of the border strips so they are exactly lined up with the edges of the quilt, crossing at right angles. If your rotary-cutting mat has a grid on it, use the grid lines to be sure your strips are at right angles. On the wrong side of the top border strip, draw the miter seam line at a 45° angle as shown. Switch the strips so the other one is on top and draw the other miter seam line on its wrong side. Pin the miter seam right sides together, matching the drawn seam lines.

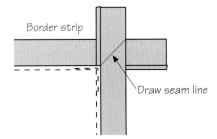

Border strip

Draw seam line

3. Sew the miter seam, starting ¼" in from the inside corner, backstitching, and sewing out to the point. Trim away all but a ¼" seam

allowance and press the seam open. Repeat on the other three corners.

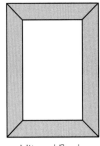

Mitered Border

MAKING THE QUILT BACKING

Backings for small quilts can be cut from a single piece of fabric. Be sure to trim off the selvages, which can draw in the edges and prevent the back from lying flat.

Although there are some 90"-wide fabrics available for quilt backings, usually you will piece the backing for a quilt wider than 40". For quilts up to 80" wide, simply piece two lengths of fabric together with a long center seam. For a quilt 50"–60" wide, you might want to add a contrasting fabric strip or pieced blocks to one side of the quilt, or cut the main piece of fabric in half lengthwise and add a strip to the center. Seams in quilt backings are usually pressed open to reduce bulk.

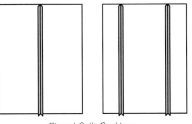

Pieced Quilt Backings

BASTING THE QUILT

Purchase packaged batting intended for hand or machine quilting. Take it out of the package the night before to allow it to relax.

1. Lay the quilt backing on the floor, wrong side up. Smooth out all wrinkles. Use masking tape around edges to hold backing in place.
2. Lay the batting on top of the quilt back, smoothing out any wrinkles. Smooth the

quilt top over the batting and pin through all the layers here and there around the edge.

3. Crawl around on the quilt and hand baste the layers together with 1" stitches, in horizontal and vertical lines about 3" apart. Always baste with white thread; colored thread may leave little colored dots when you remove it after quilting. Also baste all around the quilt about ¼" in from the edge; this will hold the edges together when you add the binding later.

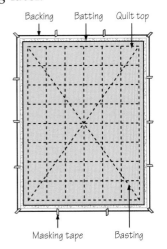

Masking tape   Basting

4. If you plan to machine quilt, you may choose to baste your quilt with safety pins rather than basting stitches. Fasten the pins about 3" apart, avoiding the lines along which you plan to quilt.

QUILTING

Quilting is the stitching that holds together the backing, batting, and quilt top. You can quilt by hand or machine.

Hand Quilting

1. Place the basted quilt in a hoop or quilting frame. Start in the center of the quilt and quilt in sections toward the edges, moving the hoop as necessary. Use short quilting needles called "Betweens" and the heavy thread sold as hand-quilting thread. You will also need a quilting thimble, which is like a regular thimble except that it is indented on the end rather than rounded out.

2. Tie a small knot in the end of the thread. With the needle, wiggle a hole in the surface

of the quilt about ½" from the place you plan to start quilting. Push the threaded needle in through the hole and back out on top of the quilt where you plan to start, pulling the knot through the hole so it is buried in the batting. There should be no knots showing on either the top or the bottom of the quilt.

3. Quilt with a running stitch. Use the quilting thimble on your third finger to push the needle through the quilt, rocking the needle up and down to help make the stitches smaller.

4. When you reach the end of your thread or a stopping place in your design, tie a knot in the thread, pull the knot into the batting, and cut the thread even with the surface of the quilt.

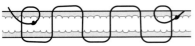

Be sure stitches go through all three layers.

Machine Quilting

Machine quilt with regular sewing thread or with the thin nylon thread made for machine quilting. If you use nylon thread, use regular thread in the bobbin. Set the machine for a stitch slightly longer than you use for regular sewing. Roll up the parts of the quilt you aren't working on to keep them out of the way. Whenever possible, start and stop at the edges of the quilt and backstitch for security; the ends will be covered by the binding. When you must start and stop in the middle of the quilt, leave 4" thread ends. When you are finished, thread each end on a needle, pull it inside the quilt through the batting, and trim on the quilt surface.

BINDING

Finish the edges of your quilt after you have quilted it, as quilting tends to pull it up and make it smaller. Almost all the quilts in this book were finished with ½" straight-grain double-fold binding.

To make ½" binding:

1. Cut strips from the binding fabric 2¾" wide. Cut enough strips to go around the quilt plus about 20" for joining the strips and turning the corners.

2. Join the strips at right angles with a diagonal seam as shown. Trim away excess, leaving a ¼"-wide seam allowance. Press seams open.

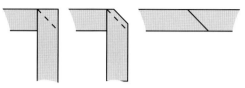

3. Trim one end to a 45° angle and press under ¼". Fold the strip in half lengthwise, wrong sides together, and press.

4. Trim the quilt so that the batting and backing extend ¼" beyond the raw edge of the quilt top. Machine sew the binding strip to the right side of the quilt, right sides together. Match the raw edges of the binding with the edges of the quilt top (not the edge of the batting and backing) and take a ¼" seam. Start with the end cut to a 45° angle and end by overlapping it with the binding strip. Stop the seam at each corner ¼" from the edge of the quilt top; backstitch.

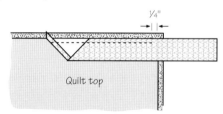

5. At the corner, fold the binding strip away from you and then back toward you as shown, lining up the fold with the top edges of the batting and backing and the raw edges of the binding aligned with the edges of the quilt top. Start sewing the next side at the edge of the fold, backstitching. Repeat at each corner.

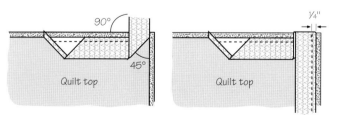

6. Fold the binding to the back of the quilt and hand stitch down. At each corner, a miter will form automatically on the front of the quilt; fold the binding to make a miter on the back.

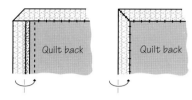

To make 1" binding:

Cut the strips 4¾" wide. Trim the batting and backing ¾" beyond the raw edge of the quilt top. Attach binding in the same manner as described above for ½" binding. You may need more yardage than what is called for if you plan to cut your strips 4¾" wide.

Straight-Corner Binding

If you don't want to miter the corners of the binding, trim the quilt as described above and sew the binding strip to the sides of the quilt, right sides together, matching the raw edges of the binding strip to the edge of the quilt top and taking a ¼" seam. Trim the binding even with the batting and backing at each end. Fold the binding to the back of the quilt and hand stitch in place.

Sew the binding to the top and bottom edges of the quilt. Turn under ¼" at each end; blindstitch the ends closed.

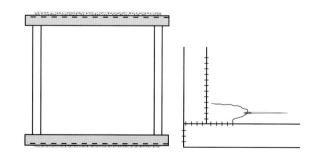

EMBROIDERY DETAILS

You can embroider details on some of the cats with the embroidery stitches shown here.

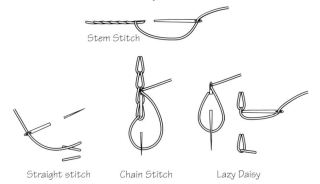

Stem Stitch

Straight stitch   Chain Stitch   Lazy Daisy

You may want to add eyes, noses, and/or whiskers to your cats. I often don't because I think they interfere with the simplicity and graphic impact of the designs. When I do add eyes, I usually make small French knots and place them close together just below the midline of the face. You can use buttons for eyes, but keep them small or they will look like goggles. Again, place them close together and just below the midline. Whiskers may be straight or may curve slightly for a more natural look.

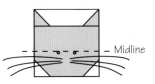

— Midline

USING CAT FABRICS

A number of wonderful fabrics printed with cats are available to quilters, and it seems as if new ones appear each month. How can you use them?

There are many traditional quilt designs in which you could feature small printed cats. Cathedral Window quilts are especially fun if animals and other unusual printed designs are framed in the little blocks. When I make almost any quilt for small children, even if I am speed piecing, I cut a few pieces one by one from animal fabrics, centering the design.

Large cat prints are more difficult to use. When used in traditional patterns, they often overwhelm the design. Cats that end up headless, tailless, or feetless are a little unsettling, but quilters used to speedy rotary cutting are not happy cutting the pieces for a quilt one by one. Centering designs can also result in a lot of bias edges where you don't want them. There is yet another problem if the cat print is directional: Should all the cats be right side up? Often, the cutting and piecing steps must be modified if a direction must be maintained.

Puss in the Center (page 21) demonstrates one approach to using a large-scale print. Puss in the Center isolates an individual cat in the center of each block. In the particular print I chose, the cats were printed close together, so to isolate the cats, I cut each out individually and appliquéd it to the block. This would not be necessary if there were more space around each printed cat.

Large-scale cat prints were used for the backs of several of the quilts in this book. The back of White Ties and Tails (below) is actually a large panel of a printed stuffed-animal kit. If your quilt top has expanses of light fabric, however, be cautious about using a bold print with a lot of dark/light contrast for the back; the dark areas may show through.

CAT APPLIQUÉS

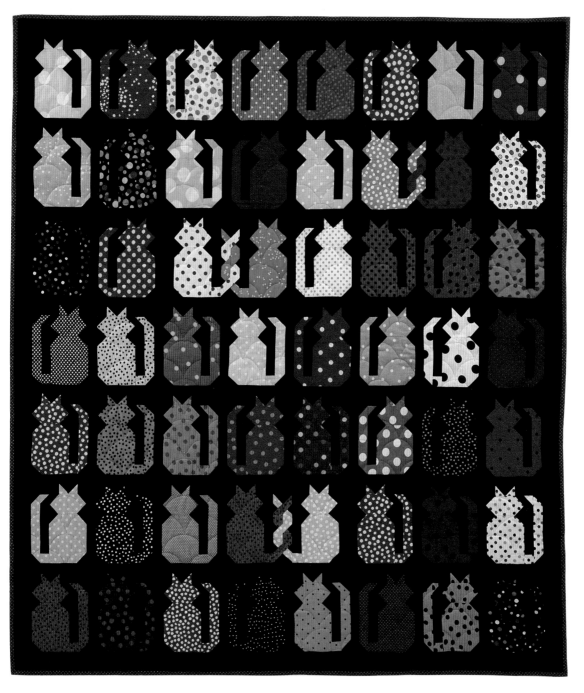

Jazz Cats by Janet Kime, 1993, Vashon Island, Washington, 59½" x 66½". Polka dots of every hue, just for fun, liven this quilt. Can you find the three pairs of sweethearts? Quilted by Marianna Garrett. (Directions on page 49.)

Kittleson's Cats by Meg Schoch, 1993, Vashon Island, Washington, 49½" x 49½". These Siamese cats seem to be surrounded by vines and leaves. (Directions on page 56.)

The Cats Who Charmed a Quilter by Janet Kime, 1993, Vashon Island, Washington, 18" x 14". Fans of mystery writer Lilian Jackson Braun will recognize Koko and Yum Yum, the companions of sleuth Jim Qwilleran, in this variation of Jazz Cats.

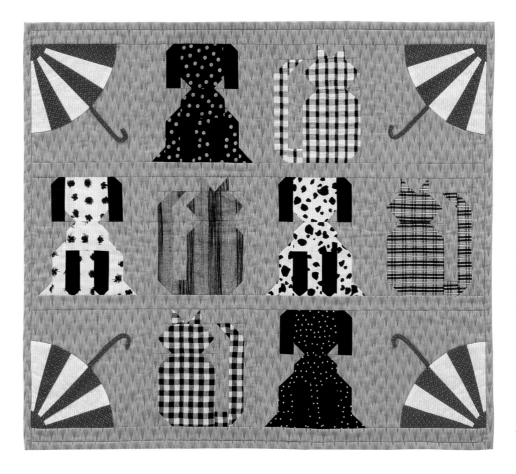

It's Raining Cats and Dogs in Seattle by Janet Kime, 1993, Vashon Island, Washington, 38" x 32". Combine cats from Jazz Cats and dogs from Firehouse Dogs, plus fans from The Motley Crew to make umbrellas, and you have a perfect picture of life in Seattle.

Firehouse Dogs by Janet Kime, 1993, Vashon Island, Washington, 24½" x 25½". Thanks to Walt Disney, dalmations are back, and one of them has a sense of humor. (Directions on page 62.)

Gallery

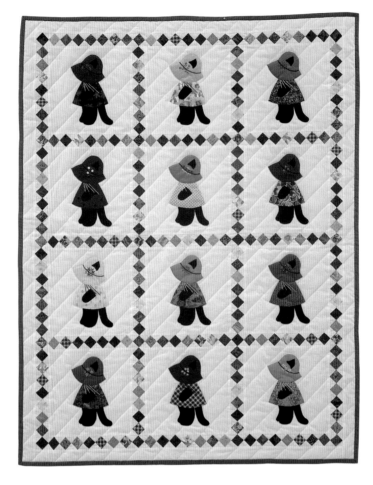

*Puss in Bonnets by
Virginia Morrison, Seattle,
Washington, 1993,
39¼" x 50½". Traditional
Sunbonnet Sue blocks—
except, wait a minute—
are those tails?
(Directions on page 66.)*

*Sunbonnet Suzy by
Marilyn Bacon, Edmonds,
Washington, 1993,
37" x 37". The reproduc-
tion 1930s and 1940s
prints available now are
perfect for Sunbonnet Sue
quilts. One of Marilyn's
cats is named Suzy,
so there was no question
about what to name this
quilt. For this Puss in
Bonnets variation,
appliqué the blocks on
point and add sashing.*

18

*White Ties and Tails
by Janet Kime, 1993,
Vashon Island,
Washington,
34½" x 16½". Four cats
are ready for an evening
on the town, although
one has his own ideas
about formal wear.
(Directions on page 53.)*

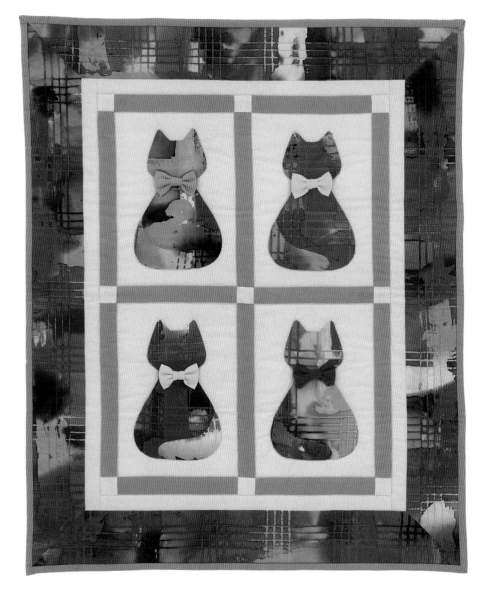

*Bow Ties by
Karen Gabriel, 1993,
Princeton Junction,
New Jersey, 25" x 31".
An unusual and striking
fabric dominates this
bright pastel variation
of White Ties and Tails.*

Checkers by Carol Kime, 1993, Battle Creek, Michigan, 41½" x 22½". Speed-pieced checkerboard cats work up quickly, here in patriotic fabrics. Quilted by Janet Kime. (Directions on page 43.)

Lancaster Cats by Joel T. Patz, 1993, Seattle, Washington, 30" x 31". These checkered cats look like folk art, especially when done in solid colors with a black background for an Amish touch.

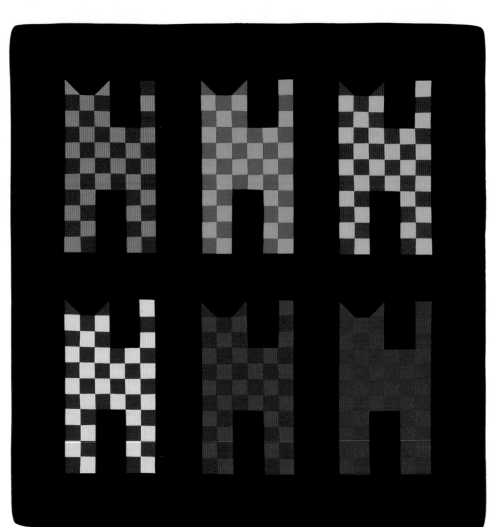

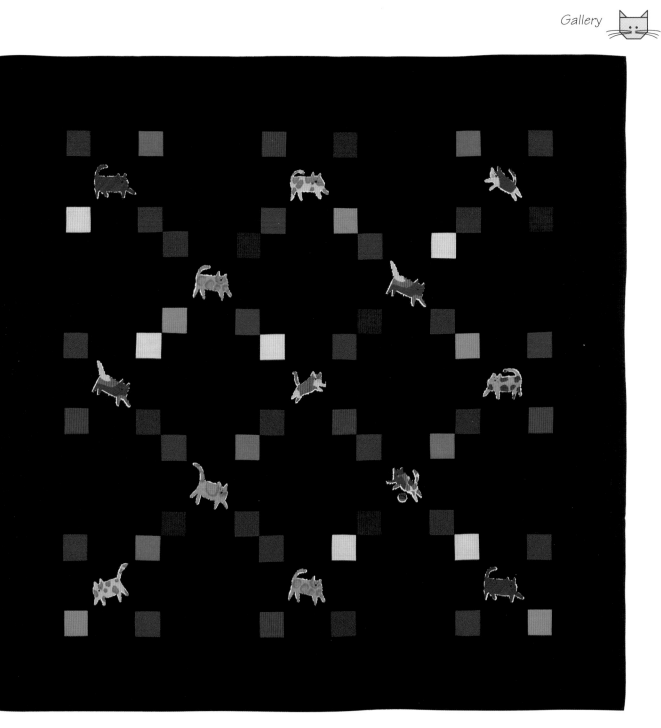

*Puss in the Center by Janet Kime, Vashon Island, Washington, 1993, 38½" x 38½".
A variation of the traditional Puss in the Corner block, this bright quilt uses
an old quiltmaking technique, broderie perse. The cats were cut from a printed
fabric and appliquéd to the centers of the blocks. (Directions on page 89.)*

*Not Just Another Kitty Face by Virginia Morrison, 1993, Seattle, Washington, 40" x 52".
Bright colors and lots of machine-quilted whiskers make this variation of
the Stealth quilt a wonderful child's quilt.*

Stealth by Janet Kime, 1993, Vashon Island, Washington, 35½" x 33½". Some of the cats you can see easily; some you have to look for. (Directions on page 41.)

Facemats by Karen Gabriel, 1993, Princeton Junction, New Jersey, 11" x 17". Another cheerful use of the cats from the Stealth quilt.

MomCats by Janet Kime, 1993, Vashon Island, Washington, 24½" x 26½". These maternal cats are sewn from dainty flower prints and lace doilies collected over the years. (Directions on page 36.)

Kelvie's Kitties by Marion Shelton, Redmond, Washington, 1993, 21" x 25½". The little white mice in the border recall the mice Marion's sister tormented her with when they were children. (Collection of Kelvie Malia Shelton. Directions on page 82.)

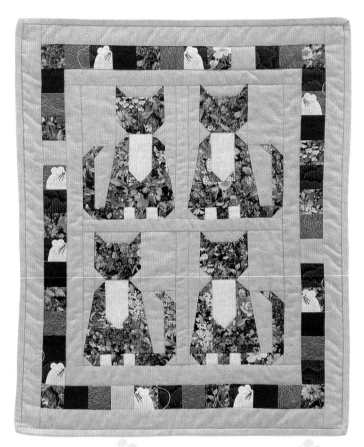

Santa Claws Is Coming to Town by Janet Kime, 1993, Vashon Island, Washington, 34½" x 22". Santa brought a cat toy for each of these good little kittens. (Directions on page 39.)

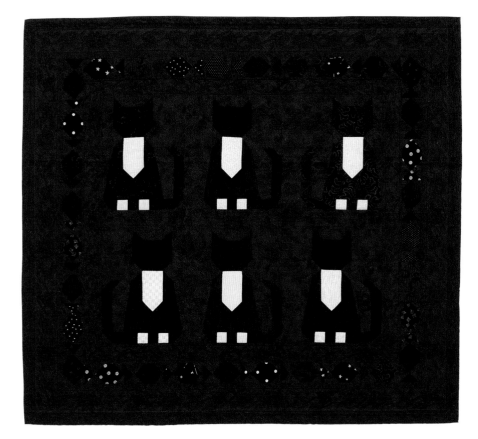

Fish Dreams by Janet Kime, Vashon Island, Washington, 1993, 32½" x 29½". Fish Dreams has the same cats as Kelvie's Kitties, but these cats have fish on their minds rather than mice. (Directions on page 87.)

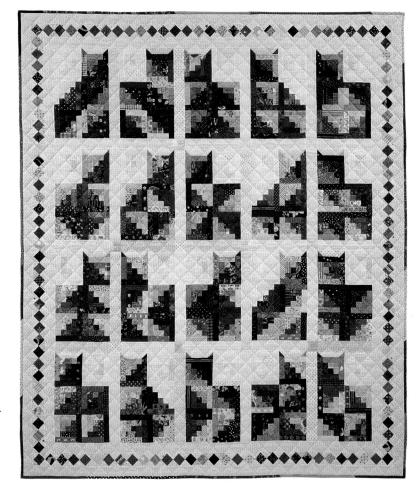

Hunter's Cats by Janet Kime, 1993, Vashon Island, Washington, 70" x 82". Use up all your leftovers to make this bed-size quilt from traditional Log Cabin blocks. (Collection of Hunter Davis, Wilson Abbott, and family.)

Four Brown Cats by Joel T. Patz, 1993, Seattle, Washington, 35½" x 47½". Joel's subtle colors and interesting set design give a new look to traditional Log Cabin blocks. (Directions on page 46.)

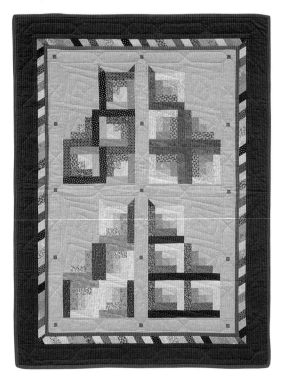

Plaid Cats by Janet Kime, 1992, Vashon Island, Washington, 50½" x 56½". Plaid cottons in warm colors, no border, and simple quilting all contribute to the home-spun, frontier look of this lap quilt. (Collection of Donna Klemka, Martin Baker, and family. Directions on page 31.)

Susan's Cats by Susan Konecki and friends, 1992–93, Vashon Island, Washington, 42½" x 48½". Susan started this quilt just before her death in a small-plane crash; it was finished by the members of her sewing group. Each fabric is used for one cat and one spool, so this child's quilt is also a matching game. (Collection of Brian Quinn. Directions on page 33.)

Sampler Cats by Janet Kime, Vashon Island, Washington, 1993, 38½" x 34½". The bodies of these vivid cats are traditional 5" pieced blocks. Quilted by Ann Guerrero. (Directions on page 74.)

Cowboy Cats by Julie Pearson, Seattle, Washington, 1993, 43½" x 36½". These six cowboy cats—three good guys and three bad guys— are all dressed up for the wild West in cowboy hats, bandannas, and chaps. (Directions on page 91.)

NOEL by Janet Kime, Vashon Island, Washington, 1993, 29" x 15". This variation of Sampler Cats is only one of many quilts and wall hangings you can make by substituting alphabet blocks for the sampler blocks. Quilted by Ann Guerrero.

A Tale of Three Kitties by Virginia Morrison and Janet Kime, Seattle, Washington, 1993, 21½" x 38½". This quick-and-easy project will warm any cat lover's heart. (Directions on page 69.)

The Motley Crew by Janet Kime, 1993, Vashon Island, Washington, 35½" x 26½". These graceful cats start as traditional Grandmother's Fans. (Directions on page 59.)

FireCats by Janet Kime, 1993, Vashon Island, Washington, 32½" x 25½". The hand-dyed fabrics almost flicker with light in this interpretation of The Motley Crew.

Plaid Cats

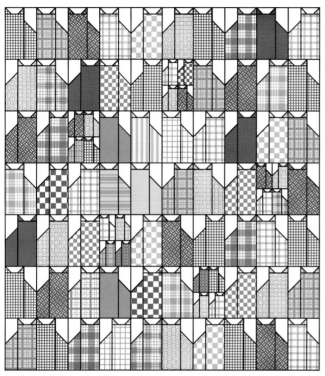

This is a very elemental Cat block with few pieces. The diagonals are all speed-pieced, making this a good project for a beginner.

Color photo:	page 27
Quilt Size:	50½" x 56½"
Finished Block Size:	Large cats 5" x 8"
	Small cats 2½" x 4"

MATERIALS: 44"-wide fabric

2½ yds. total plaid and striped fabrics for cats
1¼ yds. total plaid and striped fabrics for background
3 yds. for backing
⅝ yd. for binding

CUTTING

Note: The squares and rectangles you cut will not look like the corresponding pieces in the block diagram because all the diagonals are speed-pieced. The diagram shows you the location of each piece, not its actual shape.

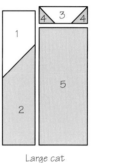
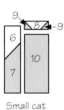

Large cat   Small cat

	Piece No.	No. of Pieces	Dimensions
Cat Fabrics			
Large cats	2	65	2½" x 6½"
	4	130	1½" x 1½"
			(2 to match each cat)
	5	65	3½" x 7½"
Small cats	7	20	1½" x 3½"
	9	40	1" x 1"
			(2 to match each cat)
	10	20	2" x 4"
Background Fabrics			
Large cats	1	65	2½" x 4½"
	3	65	1½" x 3½"
Small cats	6	20	1½" x 2½"
	8	20	1" x 2"

PIECING THE BLOCKS

Press all seam allowances in the direction of the arrows unless otherwise instructed.

1. To make the cat-back unit, sew a background 1 to a cat 2 as shown. (For small cats, speed-piece a background 6 to a cat 7.) Note that there are two ways to piece this seam.

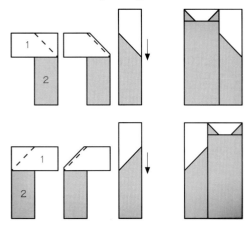

The only difference between the cats facing left and the cats facing right is the direction of the back seam.

2. To make ear units, speed-piece a cat 4 to each end of a background 3 as shown. (For small cats, speed-piece cat 9 to background 8.)

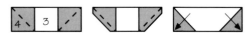

3. Sew the ear unit to the body.

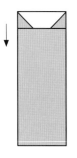

4. Sew the cat-back unit to the body.

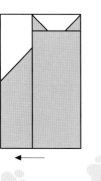

ASSEMBLING AND FINISHING THE QUILT TOP

1. Sew the small Cat blocks together in groups of 4. Press the seam allowances of each pair in opposite directions.

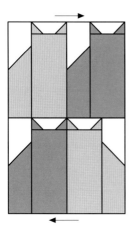

2. Arrange the large Cat blocks and small Cat blocks in 7 rows of 10 blocks each. Sew the blocks in horizontal rows; press the seam allowances in opposite directions from row to row.

3. Sew the rows together; press the seam allowances toward the top of the quilt.

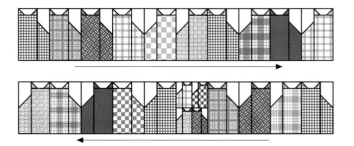

4. Layer the quilt top with batting and backing; baste.
5. Quilt as desired or in diagonal rows 2" apart.
6. Bind the edges of the quilt.

Susan's Cats

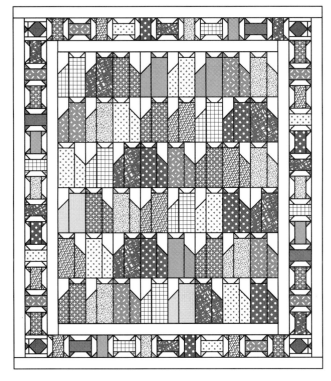

Color photo: page 27
Quilt Size: 42½" x 48½"
Finished Block Size: Cats 3¾" x 6"
Spools 3" x 3"
Fish 3" x 3"

MATERIALS: 44"-wide fabric

1½ yds. for borders and background
Scraps of 48 fabrics, or 1¼ yds. total
Scraps of a 49th fabric for 4 fish corner squares
1½ yds. for backing
½ yd. for binding

CUTTING

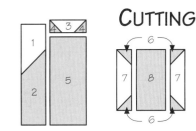
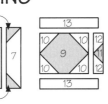

	Piece No.	No. of Pieces	Dimensions
Cat/Spool Fabrics			
Cats	2	48	2" x 5"
	4	96	1¼" x 1¼"
			(2 to match each cat)
	5	48	2¾" x 5¾"
Spools	6	192	1¼" x 1¼"
			(4 to match each spool)
	8	48	2½" x 3"
Fish Fabric			
Fish	9	4	2½" x 3"
	11	4	1" x 1½"
Background Fabric			
Cut inner and outer border strips from the lengthwise grain of the fabric first, then cut remaining background pieces.			
Inner border sides	2		2" x 39½"
Inner border top & bottom	2		2" x 30½"
Outer border sides	2		2" x 45½"
Outer border top & bottom	2		2" x 42½"
Cats	1	48	2" x 3½"
	3	48	1¼" x 2¾"
Spools	7	96	1¼" x 3½"
Fish	10	16	1½" x 1½"
	12	8	1" x 1½"
	13	8	1" x 3½"

Susan's Cats is a special quilt. Susan and her husband, John, and their friends Sarah and Richard, died in a small-plane crash. When friends went to Susan and John's house after the accident to feed their cats, they found the first eleven blocks of this quilt laid out on the floor along with Susan's shoe boxes of neatly arranged red, pink, and green fabrics. The quilt was to be photographed for this book and then given to friends who were expecting a child. Susan had not made a sketch of the quilt, although we could see that she had planned to make each cat from a different fabric, using many "conversation prints" with animals, objects, and people in the designs.

The remaining members of our little sewing group finished the quilt with Susan's and Sarah's fabrics and some of our own. The border of spools represents us, and the four fish in the corners are for John, who was just finishing his Ph.D. in fishery sciences. As I sketched the design, I realized there would be equal numbers of cats and spools. We used each fabric for one cat and one spool, so the quilt is also a matching game.

PIECING THE BLOCKS

Press all seam allowances in the direction of the arrows unless otherwise instructed.

1. Following steps 1–4 for Plaid Cats on page 32, piece 48 cats.
2. To make Spool blocks, speed-piece a spool 6 to each end of a background 7. Sew a unit to each side of spool 8.

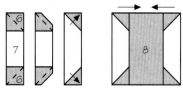

4. To make the fish body, speed-piece a background 10 to each corner of a fish 9. Sew 2 pieces to one long side, trim, and press; then sew 2 pieces to the other long side.

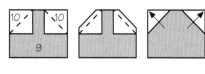

5. To make the fish tail, speed-piece a background 12 to each end of a fish 11.

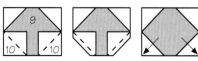

6. Sew the tail unit to the fish body. Press seam allowances open to reduce bulk.

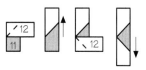

7. To complete the Fish block, sew a background 13 to the top and bottom of the fish.

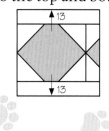

ASSEMBLING AND FINISHING THE QUILT TOP

1. Arrange Cat blocks into 6 rows of 8 blocks each. Sew the blocks in horizontal rows. Press seam allowances in opposite directions from row to row.
2. Join rows together. Press seam allowances toward the top of the quilt.
3. Sew the inner border to the top and bottom first, then to the sides of the quilt top. Press seam allowances toward the inner border.
4. Arrange Spool and Fish blocks around the quilt: 11 spools across the top and bottom, 13 spools on each side, and 1 fish at each corner. Alternate the direction of the Spool blocks as shown. Place each spool at some distance from its matching cat.
5. Sew 13 spools together as shown to make each pieced side border. Sew the pieced spool borders to the sides of the quilt top. Press seam allowances toward the inner border.

6. Sew 11 spools together to make the pieced top and bottom borders, adding Fish blocks to the ends as shown. Sew the pieced spool

borders to the top and bottom of the quilt top. Press seam allowances toward the inner border.

7. Sew the outer border to the sides first, then to the top and bottom edges of the quilt top. Press seam allowances toward the outer border.

8. Layer the quilt top with batting and backing; baste.

9. Quilt around each cat. Using heart template below, quilt a heart in the space between pairs of cats placed back to back.

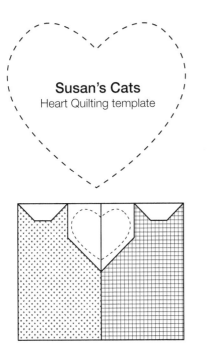

Susan's Cats
Heart Quilting template

Quilt around spools in 2 continuous lines as shown.

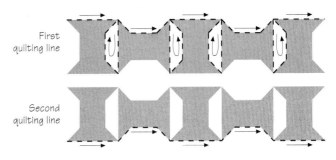

First quilting line

Second quilting line

10. Bind the edges of the quilt.

MomCats

A friend of mine with three young sons, a husband, and a thriving business tools around town in a van with "Mom Kat" license plates. One of our modern superwomen, she certainly doesn't spend her days in tiny-flowered dresses and lacy aprons, making chocolate-chip cookies and pot roasts, but her home is as full of warmth and love as that of any traditional homemaker. She might not see herself in this quilt, but I'll bet her kids can.

Color photo: page 24
Quilt Size: 24½" x 26½"
Finished Block Size: Cats 7" x 8"
Spools 2" x 2"

MATERIALS: 44"-wide fabric

¼ yd. each of 4 prints
Scraps of additional prints for spools
1 yd. for background, sashing, borders, and binding
⅞ yd. backing fabric
4 lace-edged doilies or handkerchiefs
Scraps of ribbon or bias tape for aprons
6" scraps of ⅛"-wide ribbon for bows

CUTTING

Note: The squares and rectangles you cut will not look like the corresponding pieces in the block diagram because all the diagonals are speed-pieced. The diagram shows you the location of each piece, not its actual shape.

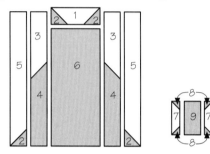

	Piece No.	No. of Pieces	Dimensions
Print Fabrics			
Cats	2	16	1½" x 1½"
			(4 to match each cat)
	4	8	1½" x 5½"
			(2 to match each cat)
	6	4	3½" x 7½"
Spools	8	168	1" x 1"
			(4 to match each piece 9)
	9	42	1½" x 2½"
Background Fabric			
Cats	1	4	1½" x 3½"
	3	8	1½" x 4½"
	5	8	1½" x 8½"
Spools	7	84	1" x 2½"
Sashing			
Vertical strips		2	1½" x 8½"
Horizontal strips		1	1½" x 15½"
Inner Border			
Sides		2	2" x 17½"
Top		1	1¾" x 18½"
Bottom		1	2¼" x 18½"
Outer Border			
Sides		2	1½" x 24½"
Top & bottom		2	1½" x 24½"

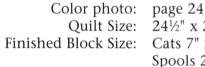

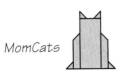

PIECING THE BLOCKS

Press all seam allowances in the direction of the arrows unless otherwise instructed.

Cat Blocks

1. To make ear units, speed-piece a cat 2 to each end of a background 1 as shown.

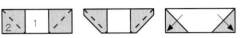

2. To make mirror-image pairs of hip units, sew a background 3 to a cat 4 as shown.

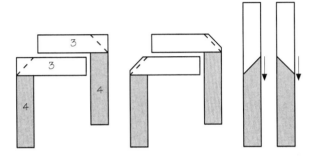

3. To make mirror-image leg units, speed-piece a cat 2 to a background 5 as shown.

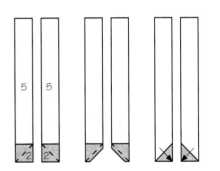

4. Sew the ear unit to one end of a cat 6.

5. Sew a hip unit to each side of the body, then add a leg unit to each side.

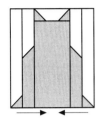

Spool Blocks

1. To make side units, speed-piece a spool 8 to each end of a background 7.

2. Sew a side unit to each side of a piece 9.

ASSEMBLING AND FINISHING THE QUILT TOP

1. Arrange Cat blocks together in 2 rows of 2 each, adding vertical sashing strips between the blocks. Sew blocks and sashing strips in horizontal rows.
2. Sew the horizontal sashing strip between the rows. Press seam allowances toward the sashing strip.

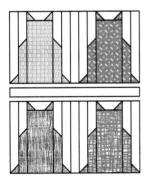

3. Sew the inner border to the sides first, then to the top and bottom edges of the quilt top. Press seam allowances toward inner border.

4. Arrange 42 Spool blocks around the edge of the quilt top: 11 each across the top and bottom, and 10 on each side. Alternate the positions of the spools as shown. Sew Spool blocks together to make pieced borders.

5. Sew the pieced borders to the sides first, then to the top and bottom edges of the quilt top. Press seam allowances toward inner border.

6. Sew the outer border to the sides first, then to the top and bottom edges of the quilt top. Press seam allowances toward outer border.

7. Layer the quilt top with batting and backing; baste.

8. Quilt around each cat and each spool; quilt the background in diagonal lines 1" apart.

9. Bind the edges of the quilt.

10. For aprons: Using the template below, cut an apron from each doily or handkerchief. Turn under ¼" along top edge and gather to fit cat body; or gather and bind top edge with ribbon or bias tape. Position apron as shown on body and hand sew to Cat block along top edge of apron.

11. Tack a ribbon bow to the neck of each cat.

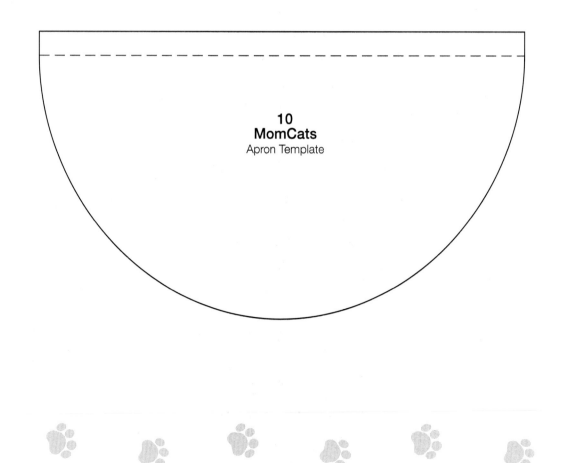

10
MomCats
Apron Template

Santa Claws Is Coming to Town

Choose a wonderful Christmas print for the border of this quilt and tuck a special toy into each kitten's Christmas stocking.

Color photo: page 25
Quilt Size: 34½" x 22"
Finished Block Size: 7" x 8"

MATERIALS: 44"-wide fabric

⅛ yd. each of 3 prints for cats
⅓ yd. for background and inner border
⅝ yd. for middle border and binding
¾ yd. for outer border
¾ yd. for backing
3 miniature wooden spools
36" of yarn
Scraps for stocking, mouse, and fish
Scraps of felt for mouse ears
Fiberfill

CUTTING

Use templates on pages 40 and 42.

Note: The squares and rectangles you cut will not look like the corresponding pieces in the block diagram because all the diagonals are speed-pieced. The diagram shows you the location of each piece, not its actual shape.

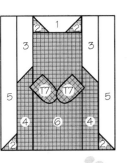

	Piece No.	No. of Pieces	Dimensions
Cat Fabrics			
Cats	2	12	1½" x 1½"
			(4 to match each cat)
	4	6	1½" x 5½"
			(2 to match each cat)
	6	3	3½" x 7½"
	T7	6	*(2 to match each cat)*
Background Fabric			
Cats	1	3	1½" x 3½"
	3	6	1½" x 4½"
	5	6	1½" x 8½"
Inner border sides		2	1½" x 8½"
Inner border top		1	1½" x 23½"
Inner border bottom		1	2" x 23½"
Middle Border Fabric			
Sides		2	1" x 11"
Top & bottom		2	1" x 24½"
Outer Border Fabric			
Sides		2	5½" x 13"
Top & bottom		2	5½" x 34½"

PIECING THE BLOCKS

1. Following steps 1–5 for MomCats on page 37, piece 3 cats.
2. Use the paper-patch method on pages 9–10 to appliqué 2 paws on each cat. See quilt plan, above left, for placement.

ASSEMBLING AND FINISHING THE QUILT TOP

1. Sew 3 Cat blocks together side by side.
2. Sew inner border to the sides first, then to the top and bottom edges of the quilt top; press seam allowances toward the border. Repeat for middle and outer borders.

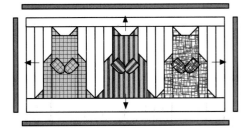

3. Layer the quilt top with batting and backing; baste.

4. Quilt around each cat and inside the middle border. Quilt holly leaves in the outer border.

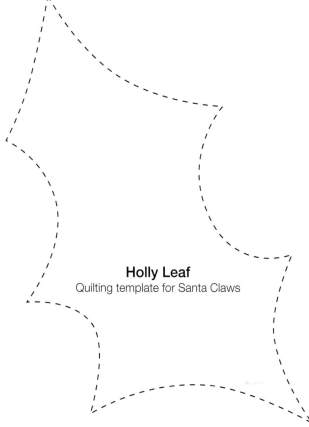

Holly Leaf
Quilting template for Santa Claws

5. Bind the edges of the quilt.

Stockings

1. Cut 2 of Template 8. Sew stockings right sides together. Clip inner curves and turn.

Clip

2. Turn top edge under ¼", then ¼" again, and hem. Attach stockings to cats where paws meet, stitching down about 1" of the stocking. Let the rest of the stocking hang free.

Toys

1. For spool toy: String spools on 12" of doubled yarn, knotting yarn between the spools and at each end.

2. For fish toy: Cut 2 of Template 9, then sew pieces right sides together, leaving 1" to turn. Stuff lightly and sew opening closed.

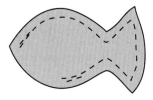

3. For mouse toy: Cut 2 of Template 10 and 2 of Template 11. Sew mouse bodies right sides together, leaving 1" open to turn. Stuff lightly and sew opening closed. Cut 2 of Template T11 from felt. Sew ears to mouse, gathering slightly at base and positioning as shown in illustration. Tack on a yarn tail.

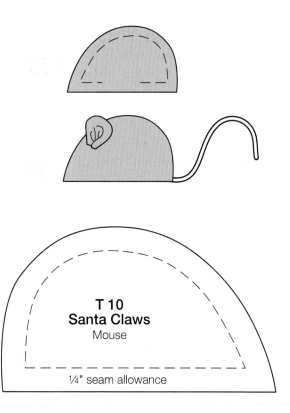

**T 10
Santa Claws**
Mouse

¼" seam allowance

Stealth

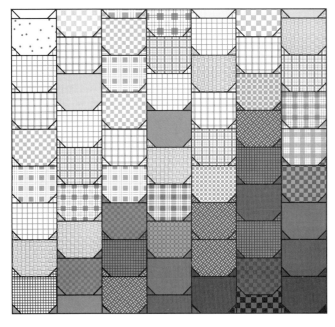

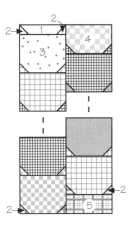

These simple interlocking cat heads piece together quickly. Each cat or portion of a cat is made from a different brown fabric, ranging from almost-white to almost-black—67 different fabrics in all. You could achieve the same effect with any similar range of colors: black and white, blues, or even a mix of colors shaded from light to dark.

Color photo:	page 23
Quilt Size:	35½" x 33½"
Finished Block Size:	4" x 5"

MATERIALS: 44"-wide fabric

Scraps of 67 fabrics OR 1¼ yds. total
1¼ yds. for backing
¼ yd. light fabric for binding
¼ yd. dark fabric for binding

CUTTING

Note: The squares and rectangles you cut will not look like the corresponding pieces in the block diagram because all the diagonals are speed-pieced. The diagram shows you the location of each piece, not its actual shape.

1. Arrange the fabrics in 7 rows:
   10 fabrics each in rows 1, 3, 5, and 7
   9 fabrics each in rows 2, 4, and 6.
2. From each of the top fabrics in rows 1, 3, 5, and 7, cut:
   1 piece, 1½" x 5½", for piece 1
3. From each of the top fabrics in rows 2, 4, and 6, cut:
   1 piece, 3½" x 5½", for piece 4
4. From each of the bottom fabrics in rows 1, 3, 5, and 7, cut:
   2 squares, each 1½" x 1½", for piece 2
5. From each of the bottom fabrics in rows 2, 4, and 6, cut:
   2 squares, each 1½" x 1½", for piece 2
   1 piece, 2½" x 5½", for piece 5
6. From each of the remaining 53 fabrics, cut:
   1 piece, 4½" x 5½", for piece 3
   2 squares, each 1½" x 1½", for piece 2

Note: As you cut out each cat, pin the ear squares (piece 2) to the matching face (piece 3) to keep them together.

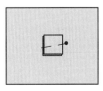

PIECING THE BLOCKS

Press all seam allowances in the direction of the arrows unless otherwise instructed.

Since each cat's ears are pieced to the cat above, you must determine the position of each cat in the quilt before you begin to piece.

1. Arrange the cats in 7 vertical rows of 10 cats each. Number the vertical rows 1–7.
2. Unpin each pair of ear squares and pin them to the cat above. Pin the ear squares of cats in the top row to each piece 1 in odd-numbered rows, and to each piece 4 in even-numbered rows.
3. Speed-piece a piece 2 to the bottom corners of a piece 3. Check to make sure that the ear fabric you are sewing to piece 3 matches the cat fabric below.

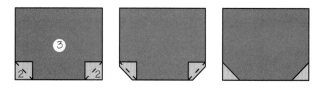

4. For the top of rows 1, 3, 5, and 7, speed-piece a piece 2 from the top row of cats to each end of a piece 1.

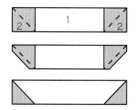

5. For the top of rows 2, 4, and 6, speed-piece a piece 2 to the bottom corners of each piece 4.

ASSEMBLING AND FINISHING THE QUILT TOP

1. Arrange the cats in 7 vertical rows, positioning the partial cats as shown in the quilt plan on page 41. Add a piece 5 to the bottom of rows 2, 4, and 6. Sew the blocks together in vertical rows, then sew rows together. Press seam allowances in one direction.
2. Layer the quilt top with batting and backing; baste.
3. Quilt around each individual cat.
4. Bind the edges with light fabric on the top and left edges, and with dark fabric on the bottom and right edges, following directions on page 13 for straight-corner binding.

Use these templates for Santa Claws Is Coming to Town on pages 39–40.

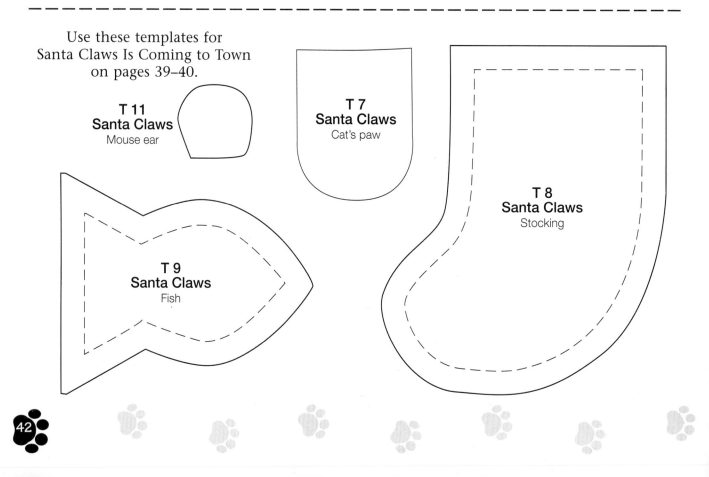

T 11
Santa Claws
Mouse ear

T 7
Santa Claws
Cat's paw

T 8
Santa Claws
Stocking

T 9
Santa Claws
Fish

Checkers

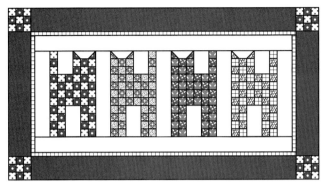

This is a simple, Template-Free®, speed-pieced pattern—simple enough to be your first foray into rotary cutting and speed piecing if you are not already converted. It's particularly important with this design to make accurate ¼" seams and to follow the pressing arrows.

Color photo: page 20
Quilt Size: 41½" x 22½"
Finished Block Size: 6" x 11"

MATERIALS: 44"-wide fabric

¼ yd. each 4 navy prints and 4 red prints
½ yd. print for background and sashing
¼ yd. for inner border
½ yd. for outer border (1¼ yds. for a length-wise stripe)
1¼ yds. for backing
½ yd. for binding

CUTTING

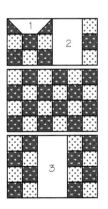

From each of the 4 navy and 4 red prints, cut:
  1 strip, 1½" x 42", for cats
From 1 navy and 1 red print, cut:
  1 strip, 1½" x 42", for corner blocks

	Piece No.	No. of Pieces	Dimensions
Background Fabric			
Cats	1	4	1½" x 3½"
	2	4	2½" x 3½"
	3	4	2½" x 4½"
Sashing			
Vertical strips		5	2½" x 11½"
Horizontal strips		2	2½" x 34½"
Inner Border Fabric			
Sides		2	1" x 15½"
Top & bottom		2	1" x 35½"
Outer Border Fabric			
Sides		2	3½" x 16½"
Top & bottom		2	3½" x 35½"

PIECING THE BLOCKS

Press all seam allowances in the direction of the arrows unless otherwise instructed.

1. Sew 1 navy strip and 1 red strip together to make a strip unit. Make 4 units.
2. Cut each strip unit in half and sew the halves together as shown to make a strip unit 4 strips high. Crosscut each strip unit into 13 segments, each 1½" wide.

1½"

3. To make the cat body, sew 6 segments together. Make 3 units as shown on the left and 1 mirror image.

Make 3.   Make 1.

4. To make leg units, sew 4 segments into 2 pairs and join to each side of a background 3. Make 3 units as shown on the left and 1 mirror image. Before sewing, check against body section to be sure checkerboard pattern is maintained.

Make 3.   Make 1.

5. From the 3 remaining segments from each strip unit, remove a navy square from 2 of the segments, and 1 red square from the third segment.

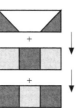

6. To make the ear unit, speed-piece the 2 navy squares removed in step 6 to each end of a background 1.

7. To make the cat head, join 2 shortened segments from step 6 and the ear unit as shown.

8. To make the head/tail unit, sew together the head section, background 2, and the remaining shortened segment. Make 3 units as shown on the left and 1 mirror image.

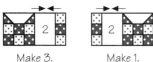

Make 3.   Make 1.

9. Sew the 3 cat sections together. Make 3 units as shown on the left and 1 mirror image.

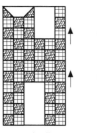

Make 3.   Make 1.

SASHING AND BORDERS

1. Arrange the Cat blocks in a horizontal row. Sew a vertical sashing strip between each block and 1 at each end of the row.

2. Sew horizontal sashing strips to the top and bottom edges of the quilt top.

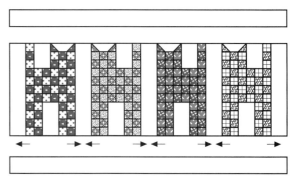

3. Sew the inner border to the sides first, then to the top and bottom edges of the quilt top; press seam allowances toward the inner border.

4. To make 4 corner blocks, cut remaining navy strip into 1 strip, 13" long, and 2 strips, each 7" long. Cut remaining red strip into 2 strips, each 13" long, and 1 strip, 7" long. Make a red-navy-red strip unit 13" long, and a navy-red-navy unit 7" long.

5. Cut 8 segments, each 1½" wide, from the long strip unit, and 4 segments, each 1½" wide, from the short strip unit.

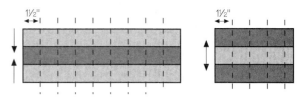

6. Assemble 4 Ninepatch blocks as shown.

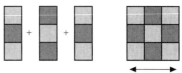

7. Sew outer borders to the top and bottom edges of the quilt top.

8. Sew the corner squares to each end of the outer side borders. Sew the side borders to

the sides of the quilt top. Press seam allowances toward the outer border.

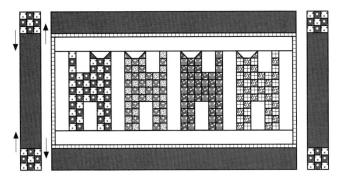

9. Layer the quilt top with batting and backing; baste.

10. Quilt around each cat and from edge to edge along the inside edge of the outer border.

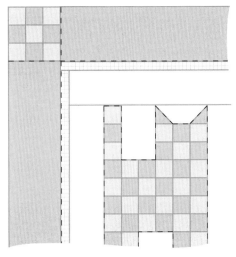

11. Bind the edges of the quilt.

Four Brown Cats

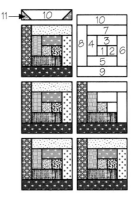

Everyone loves to make Log Cabin blocks, and now you can turn them into cats. Each cat is made from six simple Log Cabin blocks and a pair of ears. This is another quilt for your rotary cutter; with it, the logs and the striking striped border can be prepared in a matter of minutes.

Color photo: page 26
Quilt Size: 35½" x 47½"
Finished Block Size: Cats 10" x 16"
Log Cabins 5" x 5"

MATERIALS: 44"-wide fabric

¾ yd. total dark prints for cats
¾ yd. total light prints for cats
1 yd. total prints for background and sashing
¼ yd. for square dots and inner border
½ yd. for outer border
1½ yds. for backing
½ yd. for binding

From assorted light and dark prints, cut:
16 sets of light logs
20 sets of dark logs

Light Logs		Dark Logs	
Log #	Dimensions	Log #	Dimensions
2	1½" x 1½"	1	1½" x 1½"
			(center)
3	1½" x 2½"	4	1½" x 2½"
6	1½" x 3½"	5	1½" x 3½"
7	1½" x 4½"	8	1½" x 4½"
		9	1½" x 5½"

Note: In this particular quilt, each cat was made from a different group of fabrics. If you want to do the same, cut 4 sets of light logs and 5 sets of dark logs from each group of fabrics.

	Piece No.	No. of Pieces	Dimensions
Light & Dark Fabrics			
Light fabrics	11	5	1½" x 1½"
Dark fabrics	11	3	1½" x 1½"
Pieced border		16	1½" x 20"
Background Fabrics			
Cut 8 sets of light logs and cut 4 sets of dark logs, plus 8 of log 10, 1½" x 5½".			
Sashing		4	2½" x 8¼"
		6	2½" x 11¼"
		8	2½" x 9"
		4	2½" x 1¼"
Square dots		2	1" x 16"
Inner Border Fabric			
Square dots		1	1" x 16"
Sides		2	1" x 38½"
Top & bottom		2	1" x 27½"

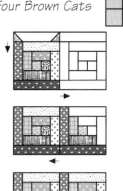

	No. of Pieces	Dimensions
Outer Border Fabric		
Sides	2	3½" x 41½"
Top & bottom	2	3½" x 35½"

PIECING THE BLOCKS

Press all seam allowances in the direction of the arrows unless otherwise instructed.

1. Piece 6 Log Cabin blocks for each cat (24 total). Starting with a square of dark fabric as the center (piece 1), add the logs in the sequence shown: 2 light, 2 dark, 2 light, 2 dark. After each seam, press seam allowances toward the log just added (toward the outside of the block) before adding the next log.

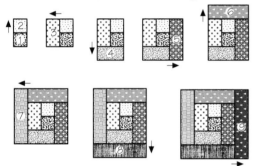

For each cat, piece the following Log Cabin blocks:

Make 4. (16 total)   Make 1. (4 total)   Make 1. (4 total)

2. To make the ear unit, speed-piece a cat 11 to each end of a background 10. Refer to the quilt plan on page 46 for placement of dark and light ears.

3. Sew the ear unit to the top of the head unit. Arrange Log Cabin blocks for each cat as shown in the quilt plan.

4. Sew each pair of Log Cabin blocks together.

5. Sew the 3 rows together. Press seam allowances in either direction.

ASSEMBLING THE QUILT TOP

1. To make square dots in sashing strips, sew a 16" background strip to both sides of a 16" inner border strip. Crosscut the strip unit into 15 segments, each 1" wide.

2. To make vertical sashing strips between cats, sew a square-dot segment between a pair of 2½" x 8¼" sashing strips. Make 2.

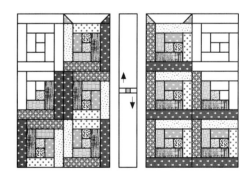

3. Sew the pieced vertical sashing strips between each pair of cats.

4. To make horizontal sashing strips, sew a square-dot segment between a pair of 2½" x 11¼" sashing strips. Make 3.

5. Sew the pieced horizontal sashing strips between the 2 rows of cats and to the top and bottom edges of the quilt top. Press seam allowances toward the sashing strips.

6. To make outer vertical sashing strips, sew the square-dot segments, 2½" x 9" sashing strips,

and 2½" x 1¼" background pieces together as shown. Make 2.

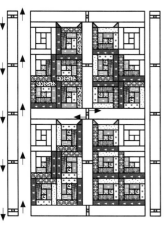

7. Sew pieced outer sashing strips to the sides of the quilt. Press seam allowances toward the sashing strips.

8. Sew inner border to the sides first, then to the top and bottom edges of the quilt top; press seam allowances toward the inner border.

9. To make pieced border, make 2 strip units of 8 strips each from the 1½" x 20" light and dark fabric strips. Stagger the strips 1" as shown. Press all seam allowances in one direction. Align the 60° line on your ruler with one of the seams in the strip unit and trim away the staggered edges. Cut 8 strips (16 total), each 1½" wide, cutting parallel to the new cut edge.

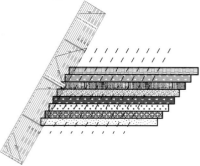

10. Sew strips together end to end to make one long pieced border strip. Be careful not to stretch the strip.

11. From the long pieced border strip, cut 2 side border strips, each 43" long, and 2 top and bottom border strips, each 32" long. Pin to the sides and the top and bottom of the quilt top, right sides together, being careful not to stretch the quilt or the border strips. The border strips should extend the same distance at each end of the quilt. Sew borders to each side of the quilt, starting and stopping ¼" in from the edges of the quilt top and backstitching for strength. Press seam allowances toward the inner border strip.

Miter the corners as shown on page 11; press miter seams open.

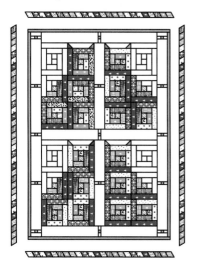

12. Sew the outer border to the sides first, then to the top and bottom edges of the quilt top; press seam allowances toward the outer border.

FINISHING

1. Layer the quilt top with batting and backing; baste.

2. Quilt each Log Cabin block in a continuous counterclockwise spiral. Quilt a corner-to-corner line diagonally across each ear strip. Quilt a 1½"-wide straight-line chain design through the sashing strips, making Xs through the center of each square dot and at each point halfway between the square dots. Quilt the same design in the outer border, making the centers of the Xs about 5" apart. Mark the outer borders in from the corners, making the center Xs closer together or farther apart as needed.

3. Bind the edges of the quilt.

Jazz Cats

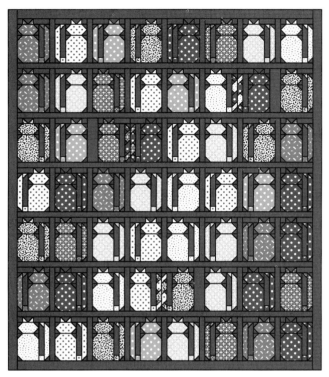

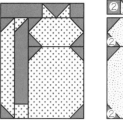

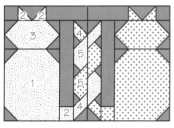

Left-tailed cat   Right-tailed cat

Entwined-tailed cats

I've been collecting polka-dot fabrics for several years now, but I didn't realize I had so many until I gathered them together for this quilt and counted up sixty-seven! Fifty-six of them were used to make the hep cats in this quilt.

      Color photo: page 15
      Quilt Size: 59½" x 66½"
Finished Block Size: 6" x 8"

MATERIALS: 44"-wide fabric

2¼ yds. total of assorted scraps for cats
3½ yds. for background, sashing, and border
4 yds. for backing
¾ yd. for binding

CUTTING

Note: The squares and rectangles you cut will not look like the corresponding pieces in the block diagram because all the diagonals are speed-pieced. The diagram shows you the location of each piece, not its actual shape.

From each of 50 cat fabrics for 50 regular Cat blocks, cut:

Piece No.	No. of Pieces	Dimensions
1	1	4½" x 5½"
2	4	1½" x 1½"
3	1	2½" x 4½"
6	1	1½" x 7½"

From each of 6 cat fabrics for 6 entwined-tailed Cat blocks, cut:

Piece No.	No. of Pieces	Dimensions
1	1	4½" x 5½"
2	3	1½" x 1½"
3	1	2½" x 4½"
4	2	1½" x 2½"
5	2	1½" x 3½"

Background Fabric
Cut borders and horizontal sashing strips from the lengthwise grain of the fabric first, then cut remaining background pieces.

	Piece No.	No. of Pieces	Dimensions
Borders			
Sides		2	2½" x 66½"
Top & bottom		2	2½" x 55½"

	Piece No.	No. of Pieces	Dimensions
Background Fabric			
Horizontal sashing strips	6		1½" x 55½"
Vertical sashing strips		46	1½" x 8½"
		3	2½" x 8½"
Cats	2	578	1½" x 1½"
	4	56	1½" x 2½"
	5	56	1½" x 3½"
	7	56	1½" x 6½"

PIECING THE BLOCKS

Press all seam allowances in the direction of the arrows unless otherwise instructed.

Make 50 regular cats, about half right-tailed and the rest left-tailed. Make 3 pairs of cats with entwined tails (56 cats total).

Regular Cats

1. To make the body unit, speed-piece a background 2 to 3 corners of a cat 1, 2 at the top and 1 at the bottom. When a corner is added to the bottom left side of the cat, the tail will be on the right; when a corner is added to the bottom right side of the cat, the tail will be on the left.

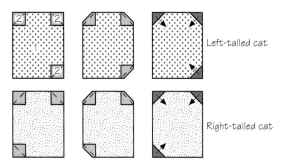

Left-tailed cat

Right-tailed cat

2. To make the head unit, speed-piece a background 2 to all 4 corners of a cat 3. Sew pieces to one long side, trim, and press; then sew pieces to the other long side.

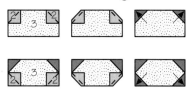

3. Sew the head unit to the body unit, matching seams and butting seam allowances against each other.

4. To make ear units, speed-piece a cat 2 to each end of a background 4. Sew, trim, and press one side before sewing the other.

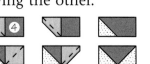

For left-tailed cats, sew a background 2 to the right side of ear unit and a background 5 to the left side. For right-tailed cats, sew a background 2 to the left side of ear unit and a background 5 to the right side. Be sure to make ear units to match right-and left-tailed cats made in step 1.

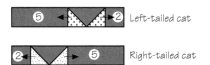

Left-tailed cat

Right-tailed cat

5. To make inner tail units, speed-piece a cat 2 to one end of a background 7. Sew a background 2 to the opposite end of cat 7. Sew as shown for right-tailed and left-tailed cats.

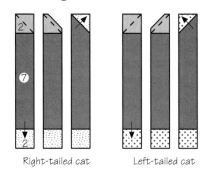

Right-tailed cat   Left-tailed cat

6. To make outer tail units, speed-piece a background 2 to each end of a cat 6.

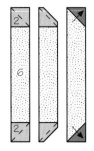

7. Sew tail units together as shown for right-tailed and left-tailed cats.

Right-tailed cat   Left-tailed cat

8. Sew tail unit to head/body unit.
9. Sew ear unit to top of block. Pin at outer edges of ears, matching head seams.

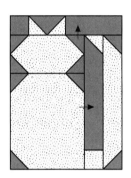

Cats with Entwined Tails

1. Following steps 1–3 above for regular cats, piece 3 pairs of cats. For each pair, make a right-tailed cat and a left-tailed cat.
2. Speed-piece a background 2 to one end of a cat 5 as shown. Make 2 identical units for each cat. For a right-tailed cat, press seam allowances toward the cat fabric. For a left-tailed cat, press seam allowances toward the background. This makes 4 long units.

Right-tailed cat   Left-tailed cat

3. For a right-tailed cat, speed-piece a background 2 to one end of a cat 4 as shown. Make 2 identical units.

Right-tailed cat

4. For a left-tailed cat, speed-piece a background 2 to each end of a cat 4 as shown. Make 2 identical units. You now have 4 long units and 4 short units.

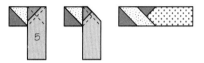

Left-tailed cat

5. Sew a long left-tailed unit to a short right-tailed unit as shown. Trim but do not press. Make 2 identical units.

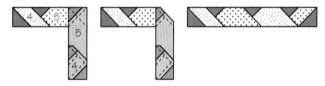

6. Sew a long right-tailed unit to a short left-tailed unit as shown. Trim but do not press. Make 2 identical units.

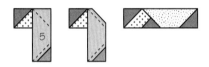

7. Sew a unit made in step 5 to a unit made in step 6 as shown. Trim but do not press. Make 2 identical units.

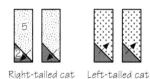

8. Lay the two identical units side by side. Turn the one on the right upside down. You should now see the entwined tails. Press seam allowances down in the left unit, and up in the right unit.

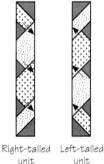

Right-tailed   Left-tailed
unit   unit

9. Sew the center seam of the entwined tails.

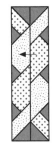

10. Sew a cat 2 to one end of a background 7. Make 2 for each pair of cats. Sew a unit to each side of a pair of entwined tails. Be sure to match cat fabrics in piece 2 to appropriate entwined tail.

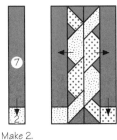

Make 2.

11. Sew the entwined tails between 2 cat head/ body units.
12. Following instructions in step 4 for regular cats, make ear units for each entwined cat.
13. Sew a pair of ear units together, then sew the ear strip to the top of the entwined cats. Press seam allowances toward the ear strip.

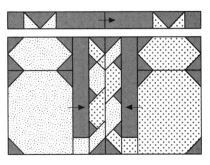

ASSEMBLING AND FINISHING THE QUILT TOP

1. Arrange the Cat blocks in 7 rows of 8 cats each, with 1½" x 8½" sashing strips between the regular Cat blocks, and a 2½" x 8½" sashing strip on one side of each pair of entwined cats.
2. Sew the blocks into horizontal rows. Press seam allowances toward the sashing strips.
3. Sew the horizontal sashing strips between each row. Press seam allowances toward the sashing strips.
4. Sew the border to the top and bottom first, then to the sides of the quilt top; press seam allowances toward the border.
5. Layer the quilt top with batting and backing; baste.
6. Quilt as desired. Jazz Cats was commercially machine quilted in a clamshell design.
7. Bind the edges of the quilt.

White Ties and Tails

	Piece No.	No. of Pieces	Dimensions
Background Fabric			
Blocks	1	4	8" x 11"
Bow Tie	7	84	1½" x 1½"
Border			
Sides		2	1½" x 14½"
Top and bottom		2	1½" x 34½"
From each black fabric, cut:			
Cats	T2	1	
	T2a	1	
	(optional)		
From the 4 black fabrics, cut:			
Bow Tie	5	42	1½" x 1½"
	6	42	1" x 1"
White Fabric			
Bow Tie	5	42	1½" x 1½"
	6	42	1" x 1"
3-D bow ties	3	3	3½" x 5½"
	4	3	1" x 1½"
Red-and-White Polka-dot Fabric			
3-D bow tie	3	1	3½" x 5½"
	4	1	1" x 1½"

These well-dressed cats are easy to appliqué. Their tails can be appliquéd as a separate piece or quilted to define the shape. The Bow Tie blocks are speed-pieced so there are no inset seams.

Color photo: page 19
Quilt Size: 34½" x 16½"
Finished Block Size: Cats 7" x 10"
Bow Ties 2" x 2"

MATERIALS: 44"-wide fabric

¼ yd. each of 4 black-on-black prints OR ½ yd. of 1 print
⅔ yd. for background and border
Scraps of white-on-white prints OR ¼ yd. of 1 print
Scrap of red-and-white polka dot for 1 of the 3-D bow ties
⅔ yd. for backing
½ yd. for binding

CUTTING

Use templates on page 55.

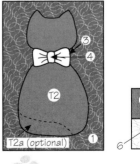

PIECING THE BLOCKS

Press all seam allowances in the direction of the arrows unless otherwise instructed.

Cat Blocks

1. Use the paper-patch method on pages 9–10 to appliqué 4 cats and 4 tails (optional) onto the background blocks. Trim the blocks to 7½" x 10½".

2. Fold piece 3 in half on the long edge, right sides together, and join the raw edges with a ¼"-wide seam. Turn inside out and tuck the raw edges of one end of the tube ¼" inside the other end; tack in place. Gather the bow in the center and hand stitch with strong thread.

3. Press under ¼" along each long edge of piece 4. Wrap the band around center of bow and tack in place on the back. Set bows aside.

Bow Tie Blocks

1. Speed-piece a white 6 to a background 7.

2. Sew a large white square to each speed-pieced square as shown.

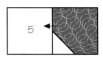

3. Sew 2 units together to make each Bow Tie block. Press seams open to reduce bulk.

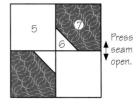

Make 21.

4. Repeat steps 1–3 with black fabric to make black Bow Tie blocks.

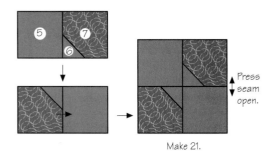

Make 21.

ASSEMBLING AND FINISHING THE QUILT TOP

1. Sew the Cat blocks into one horizontal row. Press seam allowances in either direction.
2. Alternating black-and-white Bow Tie blocks, sew together 5 blocks for each side border and 16 blocks for each top and bottom border. Press seam allowances in one direction.

3. Sew the Bow Tie borders to the sides first, then to the top and bottom edges of the quilt top; press seam allowances toward the Cat blocks.

4. Sew outer border to the sides first, then to the top and bottom edges of the quilt top; press seam allowances toward the outer border.
5. Layer the quilt top with batting and backing; baste.
6. Quilt around each cat and along upper edge of tail. Quilt along the long edges of the Bow Tie border, and quilt a diagonal line between each pair of Bow Tie blocks.

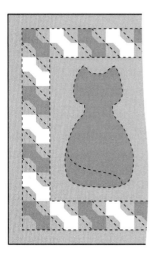

7. Bind the edges of the quilt.

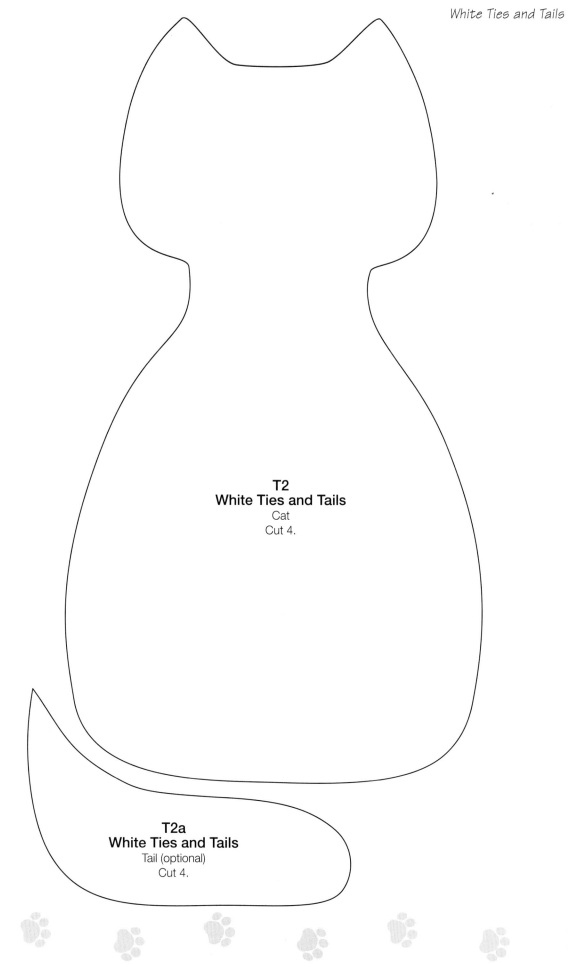

T2
White Ties and Tails
Cat
Cut 4.

T2a
White Ties and Tails
Tail (optional)
Cut 4.

Kittleson's Cats

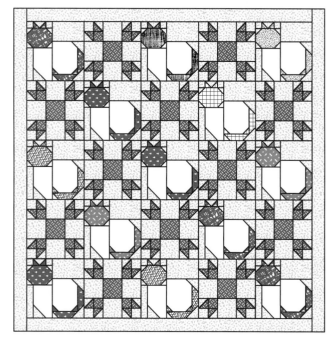

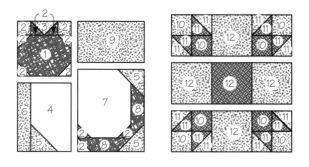

Although these Siamese Cat blocks appear complex, they are made entirely from speed-pieced squares and rectangles. The alternate Weathervane blocks lead your eye around this active design.

Color photo:	page 16
Quilt Size:	49½" x 49½"
Finished Block Size:	Cats 9" x 9"
	Weathervanes 9" x 9"

MATERIALS: 44"-wide fabric

⅛ yd. each or scraps of 13 browns
⅔ yd. cream
⅔ yd. brown for Weathervane blocks
2¼ yds. for background and border
3 yds. for backing
⅔ yd. for binding

CUTTING

Note: The squares and rectangles you cut will not look like the corresponding pieces in the block diagram because all the diagonals are speed-pieced. The diagram shows you the location of each piece, not its actual shape.

	Piece No.	No. of Pieces	Dimensions
Light Cat Fabric			
Cats	2	26	1½" x 1½"
	4	13	3½" x 5½"
	7	13	4½" x 5½"
Dark Cat Fabric			
Cats	1	13	3½" x 4½"
	2	52	1½" x 1½"
	8	26	1½" x 5½"
Weathervane Fabric			
Weather-vane blocks	10	48	2" x 2"
	11	48	2⅜" x 2⅜"
	12	12	3½" x 3½"
Background Fabric			
Cat blocks	2	65	1½" x 1½"
	3	13	1½" x 2½"
	5	39	2½" x 2½"
	6	13	1½" x 5½"
	9	13	3½" x 5½"
Weather-vane blocks	10	48	2" x 2"
	11	48	2⅜" x 2⅜"
	12	48	3½" x 3½"
Border			
Sides		2	2½" x 49½"
Top and bottom		2	2½" x 45½"

PIECING THE BLOCKS

Press all seam allowances in the direction of the arrows unless otherwise instructed.

Cat Blocks

1. To make cat head, speed-piece a background 2 to 3 corners of a dark cat 1, and a light cat 2 to the remaining corner as shown.

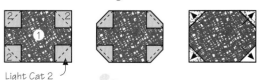

Light Cat 2

2. To make ear unit, speed-piece a dark cat 2 to each end of a background 3. Sew, trim, and press one side first before adding the other.

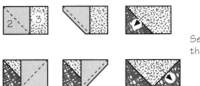

Sew one side first, then sew the other.

3. Sew a background 2 to each end of the ear unit. Sew the ear unit to the head.

4. To make the front unit, speed-piece a background 5 to a light cat 4 as shown. Sew a background 6 to the left side.

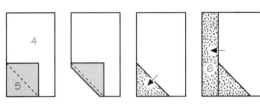

5. To make the back unit, speed-piece a dark cat 2 to the bottom corners of a light cat 7.

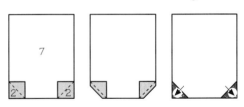

Sew a dark cat 8 to the right side of the back unit as shown. Speed-piece a background 5 to the upper right corner of the unit.

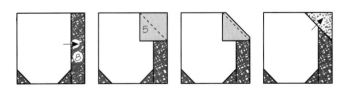

Speed-piece a light cat 2 to the left end of the dark cat 8 as shown.

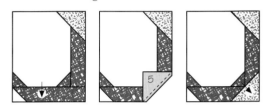

6. Sew the unit you just made to the bottom of the back unit. Speed-piece a background 5 to the bottom right corner.

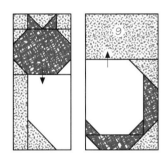

7. Sew background 9 to the top of the back unit. Sew the head unit to the front unit.

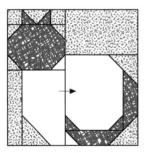

8. Sew the 2 halves of the cat together.

Make 13.

Weathervane Blocks

1. Speed-piece 48 weathervane 11 and 48 background 11 as shown to make 96 half-square triangle units. (See page 9.)

2. Sew 48 of the half-square triangle units to background 10 as shown.

3. Sew the remaining 48 half-square triangle units to weathervane 10.

4. Sew together units made in steps 2 and 3.

5. Sew the resulting unit to background 12 as shown, making 24 identical sections.

6. Sew a background 12 to each side of a weathervane 12.

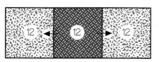

7. Assemble sections as shown to make 12 Weathervane blocks.

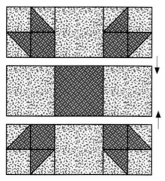

Make 12.

ASSEMBLING AND FINISHING THE QUILT TOP

1. Arrange the blocks into 5 rows of 5 blocks each, alternating the Cat and Weathervane blocks as shown in the quilt plan on page 56. Press seam allowances toward the Cat blocks.
2. Sew the horizontal rows together. Press all seam allowances in one direction.
3. Sew the border to the top and bottom first, then to the sides of the quilt top; press seam allowances toward the border.
4. Layer the quilt top with batting and backing; baste.
5. Quilt around each cat body, head, and tail. Quilt the hind leg in each cat as shown. Quilt diagonal lines through the centers of the Weathervane blocks and quilt a square within each Weathervane block.

6. Bind the edges of the quilt.

58

The Motley Crew

These motley marmalade cats are made from a number of gold fabric scraps. Even the background fabrics are a collection of white-on-muslin prints. The body of each cat is a traditional Grandmother's Fan block, and the heads and tails overlap neighboring blocks and borders.

Color photo:	page 30
Quilt Size:	35½" x 26½"
Finished Block Size:	6" x 9"

MATERIALS: 44"-wide fabric

Scraps of gold prints for cats
Scraps of white-on-muslin for background
¼ yd. for inner border
1 yd. for outer border and binding
1 yd. for backing
Embroidery floss

CUTTING

Use templates on page 61.

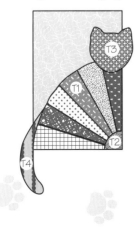

	Piece No.	No. of Pieces	Dimensions
Print Fabrics			
Cats	T1	24	
	T2	4	
	T3	4	
	T4	4	
Background Fabric			
		4	6½" x 9½"
		2	4½" x 12½"
		1	4½" x 24½"
		2	2½" x 17½"
		1	2½" x 28½"
Inner Border Fabric			
Sides		2	1" x 19½"
Top & bottom		2	1" x 29½"
Outer Border Fabric			
Sides		2	3½" x 20½"
Top & bottom		2	3½" x 35½"

PIECING THE BLOCKS

Press all seam allowances in the direction of the arrows unless otherwise instructed.

1. Sew 6 rays (T1) together to make a fan.
2. Turn under and baste ¼" along the long curved edge of each fan. Press.

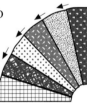

3. Position each fan on a 6½" x 9½" background rectangle, matching the raw edges of the fan with the edges of the background piece. Position 2 of the fans on the left and 2 on the right. Pin in place.
4. Appliqué the curved edge of the fans, leaving 3" at the base open so tails can be tucked under the edge later. Remove basting; press.

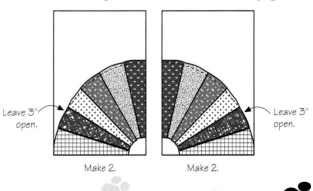

Leave 3" open.   Leave 3" open.

Make 2.   Make 2.

5. Paper-patch 4 fan bases, turning under only the curved edge. (See pages 9–10.) Pin each fan base in the bottom corner of a Fan block and appliqué the curved edge.

Fan base

6. Paper-patch 4 cat heads and 4 cat tails; set them aside. Do not turn under the insertion edge of the tail.

ASSEMBLING AND FINISHING THE QUILT TOP

1. Sew 2 pairs of cats together as shown. Appliqué the heads of the outside cats.

2. Add one 4½" x 12½" background piece to the bottom of the 2 left cats and to the top of the 2 right cats. Slipping the base of the tail under the fan, appliqué the left center tail, leaving a small portion free to remove the paper. Remove the paper from the tail, then appliqué the remainder of the tail.

Appliqué tail.

3. Sew the left cats to the right cats. Appliqué the heads of the center cats.

4. Add the 4½" x 24½" background piece to the bottom of the quilt. Slip the base of the tail under the fan and appliqué the right center tail. Remove the paper from the tail, then appliqué the remainder of the tail. Add the 2½" x 17½" background pieces to the sides of the quilt top. Then add the 2½" x 28½" background piece to the top.

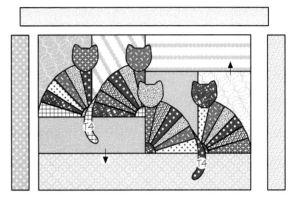

5. Appliqué the remaining tails. Remember to leave a small portion of the tail free so you can remove the paper; then finish the tail.

6. Add the inner border to the sides first, then to the top and bottom edges of the quilt top; press seam allowances toward inner border. Repeat with outer border.

7. Layer the quilt top with batting and backing; baste.

8. Quilt around each cat body and tail, and around each cat head. Quilt the background in diagonal lines 2" apart.

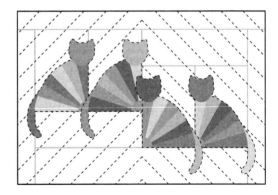

9. Bind the edges of the quilt.

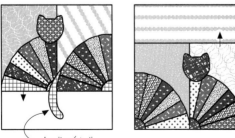

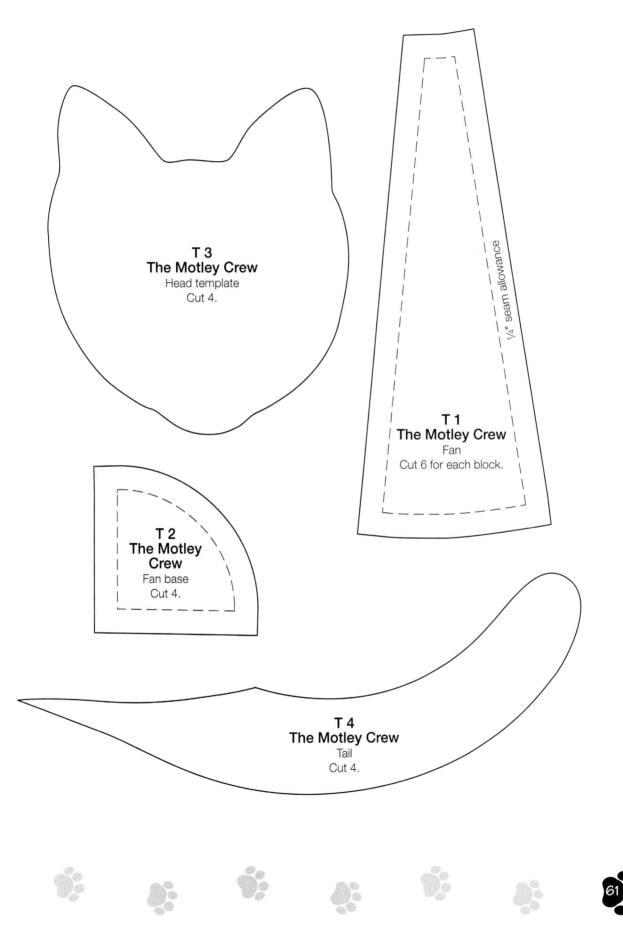

T 3
The Motley Crew
Head template
Cut 4.

T 1
The Motley Crew
Fan
Cut 6 for each block.

¼" seam allowance

T 2
The Motley Crew
Fan base
Cut 4.

T 4
The Motley Crew
Tail
Cut 4.

Firehouse Dogs

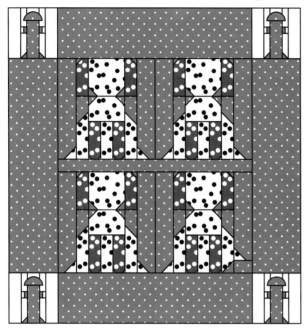

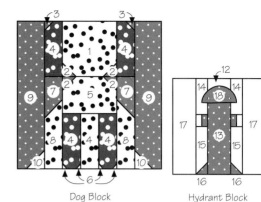

Dog Block   Hydrant Block

Here's one for the dog lovers among us. Although the block looks like it should have a lot of strange templates, it's all speed-pieced from squares and rectangles.

Color photo:	page 17
Quilt Size:	24½" x 25½"
Finished Block Size:	Dogs 8" x 8"
	Hydrants 4" x 4"

MATERIALS: 44"-wide fabric

¼ yd. light (black dots on white) for dogs
½ yd. dark (white dots on black) for dog ears, forelegs, and binding
Scraps of white fabric for corner blocks
⅔ yd. for background, sashing, borders, and hydrants
1 yd. for backing

CUTTING

Use template on page 65.

Note: The squares and rectangles you cut will not look like the corresponding pieces in the block diagram because all the diagonals are speed-pieced. The diagram shows you the location of each piece, not its actual shape.

	Piece No.	No. of Pieces	Dimensions
Light Fabric			
Dogs	1	4	3½" x 3½"
	4	4	1½" x 3½"
	5	4	2½" x 3½"
	6	16	⅞" x ⅞"
	8	8	1½" x 4¼"
	10	8	1½" x 1½"
Dark Fabric			
Dogs	4	16	1½" x 3½"
Background Fabric			
Dogs	2	16	1¼" x 1¼"
	3	8	1" x 1"
	7	8	1½" x 2¾"
	9	8	2" x 8½"
Dog with lifted leg	10	1	1½" x 1½"
	11	1	1½" x 2"
Hydrants	13	4	1½" x 3½"
	16	8	1" x 1"
	T18	4	
		1	¾" x 9"
Sashing		1	1½" x 16½"
Side borders		2	4½" x 17½"
Top & bottom borders		2	4½" x 16½"
White Fabric			
Hydrants	12	4	1½" x 1½"
	14	8	1" x 2"
	15	8	1" x 2½"
	17	8	1½" x 4½"
		1	¾" x 9"

PIECING THE BLOCKS

Press all seam allowances in the direction of the arrows unless otherwise instructed.

Dog Blocks

All 4 dogs are pieced the same through step 10. For the dog with a lifted leg, omit steps 11–12 and continue with step 13.

1. To make the head unit, speed-piece a background 2 to the bottom corners of a light 1.

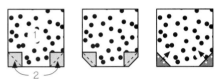

2. To make the ear unit, speed-piece a background 3 to top corners of a dark 4 as shown.

3. Sew an ear unit to each side of the head unit.

4. To make the body, speed-piece a background 2 to the top corners of a light 5.

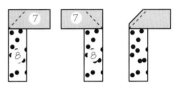

5. To make the foreleg unit, speed-piece a light 6 to the bottom corners of a dark 4.

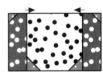

Make 2 for each dog.

6. Sew a foreleg unit on each side of a light 4.

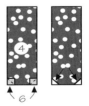

7. Sew the foreleg units to the body unit.

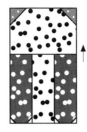

8. To make the back leg unit, speed-piece a background 7 to a light 8. Piece 4 mirror-image pairs as shown.

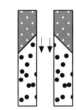

Make 1 pair for each dog.

9. Sew a back leg unit to each side of the foreleg/body unit.

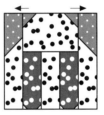

10. Sew the body unit to the head unit.

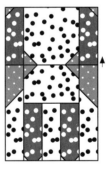

11. To make back foot units, speed-piece light 10 to background 9. Make 4 mirror-image pairs as shown.

Note: If you intend to make a dog with a lifted leg, make only 3 mirror-image pairs, plus 1 left back foot. (See steps 13–15.)

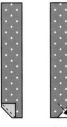
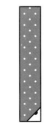

Make 1 pair for each dog.   *Make 1 extra left leg.*

12. Sew a pair of back foot units to opposite sides of 3 dogs.

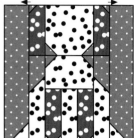

13. For the dog with lifted leg, speed-piece a background 10 to the bottom of the right hind leg as shown.

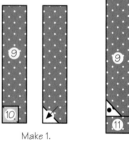

14. Trim 1 background 9 piece to 2" x 7½". Speed-piece a light 10 to the shortened background 9 as shown. Sew background 11 to the bottom of the foot.

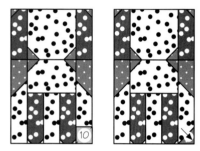

Make 1.

15. Sew the right lifted leg to the right side of the remaining dog, and a regular foot unit to the left side.

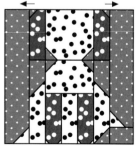

Fire Hydrant Blocks

1. To make the hydrant center, sew a white 12 to a background 13.

2. Sew the ¾" x 9" white strips and background strips together. Cut the strip unit into 8 segments, each 1" wide.

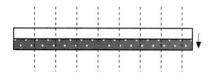

3. Sew a white 14 and 15 to each end of a 1" segment. Make 4 mirror-image pairs as shown.

Make 4 of each.

4. Speed-piece a background 16 to the end of a white 15 as shown. Make 4 mirror-image pairs as shown.

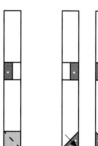

5. Sew a strip to each side of the hydrant center.

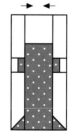

6. Sew a white 17 to each side of the hydrant.

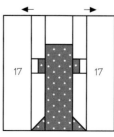

7. Paper-patch the hydrant top T18, below. Position on top of hydrant and appliqué in place.

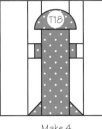

Make 4.

ASSEMBLING AND FINISHING THE QUILT TOP

1. Sew the Dog blocks together in 2 rows of 2 blocks each.
2. Sew the background sashing strip between the 2 rows of dogs. Press seam allowances toward the sashing strip.
3. Sew the 4½" x 17½" border strips to the sides of the quilt. Press seam allowances toward the borders.
4. Sew a Hydrant block to each end of the 4½" x 16½" border strips. Press seam allowances toward the borders. Sew the border strips to the top and bottom edges of the quilt top. Press seam allowances toward the borders.

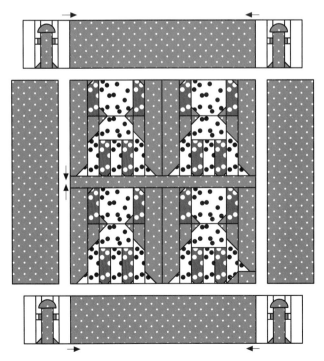

5. Layer the quilt top with batting and backing; baste.
6. Quilt around each dog and around the dog forelegs. Quilt around each Hydrant block. Quilt dog bones in the borders, 3 on each side.

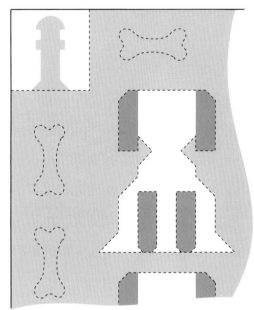

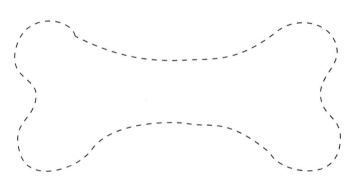

7. Bind the edges of the quilt.

T18
Firehouse Dogs
Hydrant top

Puss in Bonnets

These sunbonnet cats are hand appliquéd and make a good carry-along project. The squares-on-point sashing strips are speed-pieced.

Color photo:	page 18
Quilt Size:	39¼" x 50½"
Finished Block Size:	10" x 10"

MATERIALS: 44"-wide fabric

¼ yd. black for cats
Scraps of 12 or more prints for dresses and pieced sashing strips
Scraps of 12 coordinating solid colors for sunbonnets
1¾ yds. for background and borders
½ yd. for binding
1⅔ yds. for backing
Embroidery floss for whiskers, hatbands, and flowers

CUTTING

Use templates on pages 68.

	Piece No.	No. of Pieces	Dimension
Cat Fabric			
Cats	T1	12	
	T2	12	
	T3	12	
	T5	12	
	T7	12	
Dress Fabric			
Dress	T4	12	
Pieced border		17	1½" x 21"
Bonnet Fabric			
Bonnet	T6	12	
Background Fabric			
Cut borders from lengthwise grain of the fabric, then cut the remaining background pieces.			
Side borders		2	2" x 50½"
Top & bottom borders		2	2" x 36¼"
Blocks		12	11" x 11"
Pieced borders		34	1¾" x 21"
		30	1½" x 2"

APPLIQUÉING THE BLOCKS

Press all seam allowances in the direction of the arrows unless otherwise instructed.

1. Use the paper-patch method described on pages 9–10 to prepare appliqué pieces for sunbonnet cats.
2. Find the center of the background square by folding it in half once, then in half again.

Finger-press the creases to mark the center. Unfold the square.

3. Place the background square over the full-size drawing of the sunbonnet cat on page 68, matching the center crease with the dot. With a pencil, lightly mark the position of the legs, tail, bonnet, and dress on the background square.

4. Appliqué the pieces to the background squares in numerical order: back leg (T1), front leg (T2), tail (T3), dress (T4), arm (T5), bonnet (T6), ear (T7).

5. Embroider the whiskers, bonnet ribbons, and flowers on the bonnets (optional).

6. Press the blocks and trim to 10½" x 10½".

Speed-Pieced Sashing and Inner Border

1. Using the 21" strips of dress fabric and background fabric, sew a background strip on each side of a dress strip as shown to make 17 strip units.

2. Cut the strip units into a total of 237 segments, each 1½" wide.

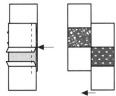

3. Sew the segments together, offsetting them as shown and butting the seam allowances against each other.

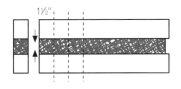

Selecting prints randomly, make the following pieced sashings and borders:

    8 strips of 7 segments each
    5 strips of 23 segments each
    2 strips of 33 segments each

4. Sew a 1½" x 2" background piece to the ends of each strip as shown. Press seam allowances all in one direction.

5. Trim the pieced strips with your rotary cutter and ruler. Lay one strip on the cutting mat as straight as possible. Align the ¼" line on your ruler on the corners of the print squares. Cut off the excess, leaving a ¼"-wide seam allowance from the corners of the squares to the edge of the strip. If necessary, cut only a few inches at a time and then reposition the ruler. Trim the other side and both ends in the same manner. Repeat for each pieced strip.

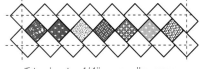

Trim, leaving 1/4" seam allowance

    Handle strips very carefully after trimming; all the edges are on the bias and can easily stretch out of shape.

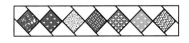

Assembling and Finishing the Quilt Top

1. Sew the short pieced strips between the Sunbonnet blocks, making 4 rows of 3 blocks each. If necessary, ease strips to fit; because all edges are bias, they will readily stretch or gather slightly.

2. Sew the 23-segment horizontal strips between the rows and to the top and bottom edges of the quilt. Press seam allowances toward the blocks.

3. Sew the 2 remaining pieced strips to the sides of the quilt.

4. Sew the outer border to the top and bottom edges first, then to the sides of the quilt top. Press seam allowances toward outer border.

5. Layer the quilt top with batting and backing; baste.

6. Quilt around the cats. Quilt diagonal lines 2" apart over the rest of the quilt; do not quilt diagonal lines through the cats.

7. Bind the edges of the quilt.

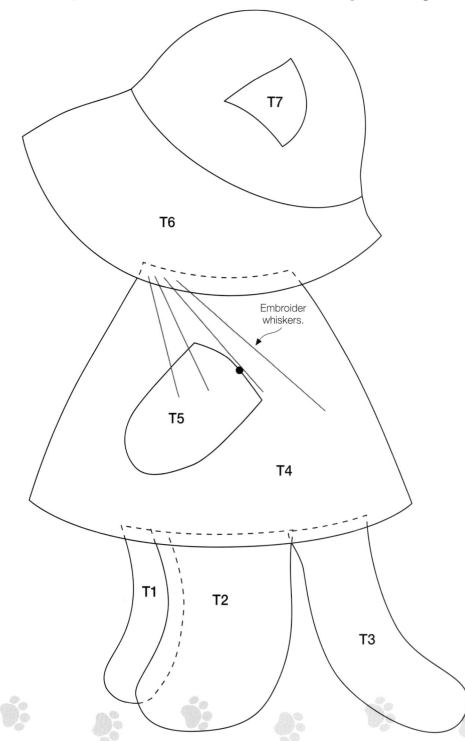

Embroider whiskers.

A Tale of Three Kitties

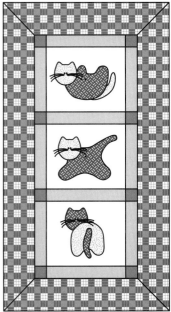

	Piece No.	No. of Pieces	Dimension
Dark Cat Fabric			
Cats	T2	1	
	T3	1	
	T4	1	
	T6	1	
Medium Cat Fabric			
Cats	T1	1	
	T3	2	
	T5	1	
Background Fabric			
Blocks		4	9" x 11"
Cut borders from the lengthwise grain of the fabric.			
Outer side border		2	4½" x 42½"
Outer top & bottom border		2	4½" x 25½"
Sashing Fabric			
Vertical strips		6	2" x 8½"
Horizontal strips		4	2" x 10½"
Cornerstone Fabric			
Cornerstones		8	2" x 2"

Kittens can't seem to strike a pose that isn't sweet. These simple appliqué cats remind me of the roly-poly little buddies that all too briefly brighten our lives.

Color photo:	page 29
Quilt Size:	21½" x 38½"
Finished Block Size:	10" x 8"

MATERIALS: 44"-wide fabric

¼ yd. medium fabric for cats
¼ yd. dark fabric for cats
⅓ yd. for background
½ yd. for sashing and binding
⅛ yd. OR scraps for cornerstones
1¼ yds. for border
¾ yd. for backing
3 yds. yarn
Contrasting embroidery floss

CUTTING

Use templates on pages 71–73.
Refer to the color photograph on page 29 for placement of the medium and dark cat fabrics.

APPLIQUÉING THE BLOCKS

Use the paper-patch method on pages 9–10 to prepare appliqué pieces. Find the center of the background rectangles by folding them in half once, then in half again. Finger-press the creases to mark the center. Unfold the piece.

Kitten with Yarn Ball

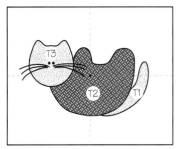

1. Paper-patch appliqué templates T1, T2, and T3.
2. Align the center dot on Template T2 with the center crease and pin in position. Tuck the tail under the body and appliqué in place.
3. Appliqué the body, then the head.
4. Following the diagram on Template 3, embroider the eyes, eyebrows, and whiskers.

Kitten Running

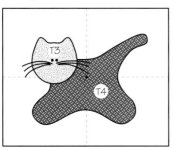

1. Paper-patch appliqué templates T3 and T4.
2. Center the body on the background and appliqué in place, then appliqué the head.
3. Following the diagram on Template T3, embroider the eyes and whiskers. Omit the eyebrows from this kitty.

Kitten Leaving

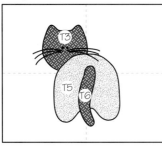

1. Paper-patch appliqué templates T3, T5, and T6.
2. Center the body on the background and pin in place. Tuck the head under the body and appliqué in place.
3. Appliqué the body, then the tail.
4. Following the diagram on Template 3, embroider the eyes and whiskers. Omit the eyebrows from this kitty.

ASSEMBLING AND FINISHING THE QUILT TOP

1. Trim the blocks to 8½" x 10½".
2. Sew the 2" x 10½" horizontal sashing strips between the blocks and to the top and bottom edges as shown above right.
3. Sew the 2" x 8½" vertical sashing strips and cornerstones together as shown to make 2 side sashing strips.

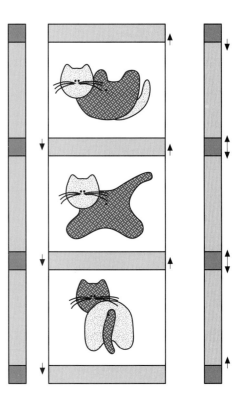

4. Sew the side sashing strips to the quilt top.
5. Sew the outer border strips to the quilt top, following directions on page 11 for borders with mitered corners. Press seam allowances toward the outer border.
6. Layer the quilt top with batting and backing; baste.
7. Quilt around each cat piece and along the inside and outside edges of the sashing strips. Quilt straight lines or a cable design in the border if desired.
8. Using a long soft-sculpture needle, "sew" yarn around the body and the feet of the kitten with the yarn ball. Make a small ball from remaining yarn and tack to the block. Run the end of the yarn into the ball and fasten. Refer to the color photo on page 29.
9. Bind the edges of the quilt.

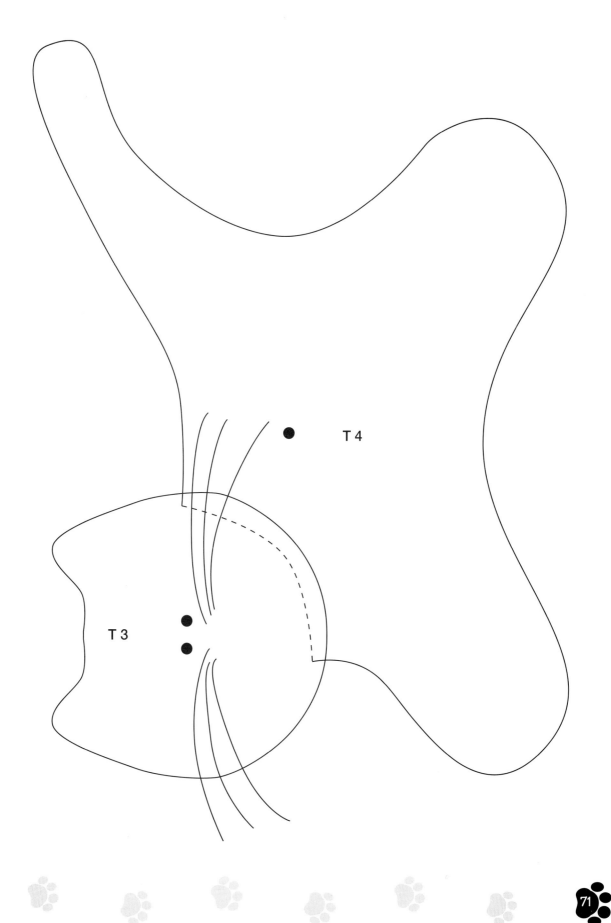

T 4

T 3

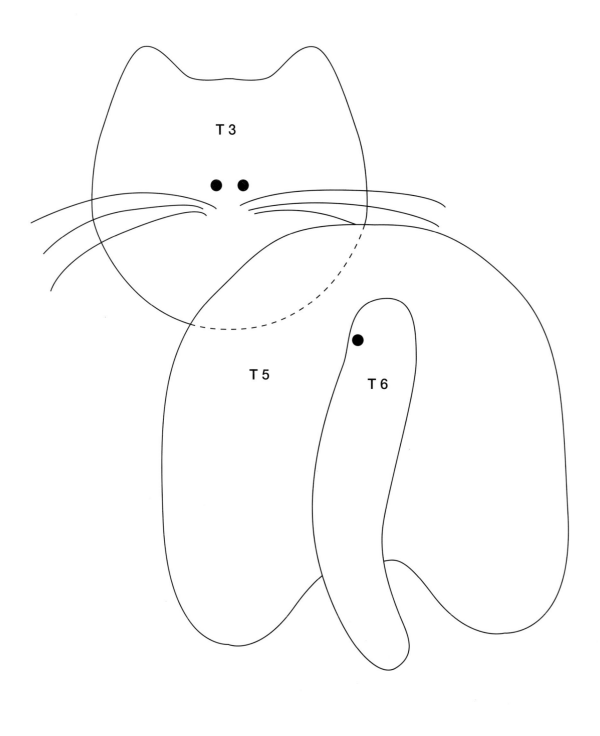

T 3

T 5

T 6

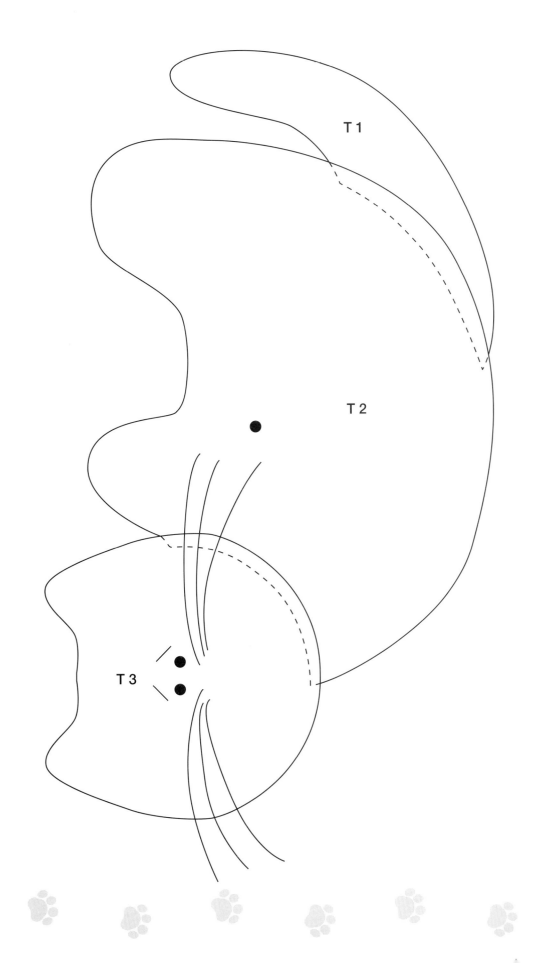

T 1

T 2

T 3

Sampler Cats

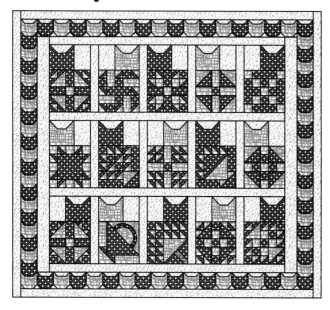

Traditional 5" quilt blocks are converted into cats in this wall hanging, which even has a border of cats. The blocks are not difficult, but the pieces are small, so your sewing must be precise. Select two colors with relatively low contrast for the Sampler blocks; you want to be able to see the different designs, but from a distance, the cats should look solid and not like Swiss cheese.

Use alphabet or number blocks on page 81 to make cat bodies spell out a name or a greeting, such as WELCOME.

Color photo:	page 28
Quilt Size:	38½" x 34½"
Finished Block Size:	5" x 8"

MATERIALS: 44"-wide fabric

1¼ yds. dark
1¼ yds. medium
1¼ yds. for background, sashing, and borders
1¼ yds. for backing
½ yd. for binding

CUTTING

Use template on page 85.

Note: Some of the squares and rectangles you cut may not look like the corresponding pieces in the block diagrams because some of the diagonals are speed-pieced. The diagrams show you the location of each piece, not necessarily its actual shape.

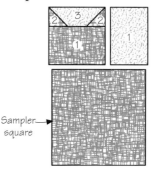

Sampler square

Border block

	Piece No.	No. of Pieces	Dimension
Dark Fabric			
Cat heads	1	8	2½" x 3½"
	2	16	1½" x 1½"
Pieced cat border	4	37	2" x 2½"
	5	74	1" x 1"
Medium Fabric			
Cat heads	1	7	2½" x 3½"
	2	14	1½" x 1½"
Pieced cat border	4	37	2" x 2½"
	5	74	1" x 1"
Background Fabric			
Cat blocks	1	15	2½" x 3½"
	3	15	1½" x 3½"
Vertical sashing strips		12	1½" x 8½"
Horizontal sashing strips		4	1½" x 29½"
Inner border sides		2	2" x 28½"
Inner border top & bottom		2	1½" x 29½"
Pieced cat border	5	68	1" x 1"
	6	34	1" x 2½"
Outer border sides		2	1½" x 34½"
Outer border top & bottom		2	1½" x 36½"

PIECING THE BLOCKS

Press all seam allowances in the direction of the arrows unless otherwise instructed.

Large Cat Heads

1. To make ear units, speed-piece a dark 2 to each end of a background 3. Make 8 ear units with dark ears and 7 with medium ears.

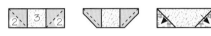

2. Sew ear unit to matching head 1.

3. To complete the head unit, sew a background 1 to one side of the head. The head unit should be on the right in about half of the blocks, and on the left in the remainder. Set head units aside.

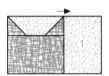

Pieced Blocks

1. Follow the step-by-step piecing diagrams on pages 77–81 to make 15 Sampler blocks.

   For the Pine Tree, press under ¼" on long edges of piece 11 and trim to match raw edges of triangle. Pin trunk in place on dark triangle. Snip seam and pull out a few stitches, then tuck end of trunk into the seam. Hand sew the seam closed and appliqué the trunk.

   For the Basket, paper-patch piece 16. Pin handle in place on medium triangle. Snip seam and pull out a few stitches, then tuck ends of basket handle into the seam. Hand sew seam closed and appliqué handle.

2. Sew the head units to the Sampler blocks. Press seam allowances in the direction of least resistance.

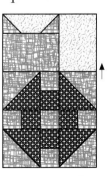

ASSEMBLING AND FINISHING THE QUILT TOP

1. Arrange the Cat blocks in 3 rows of 5 blocks each. Sew blocks together in horizontal rows with vertical sashing strips between the blocks. Press seam allowances toward the sashing strips.

2. Sew the horizontal sashing strips between the rows and to the top and bottom edges of the quilt top. Press seam allowances toward the sashing strips.

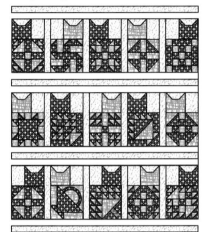

3. Sew the inner border to the top and bottom edges first, then to the sides of the quilt top. Press seam allowances toward the inner border.

4. For pieced cat border, speed-piece a medium or dark 5 to each end of background 6 to make ear units. Make 17 ear units with dark ears and 17 with medium ears.

5. Sew ear units to matching head 4.

6. Speed-piece the opposite-color piece 5 to the bottom corners of 1 dark head and 1 medium head for the top corner blocks.

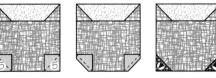

Make 1 dark.
Make 1 medium.

7. Speed-piece a background 5 to the bottom corners of 16 dark heads and 16 medium heads. Sew the heads into 2 strips of 16 each, beginning both strips with a dark head and alternating medium and dark heads as shown. Press seam allowances open to reduce bulk.

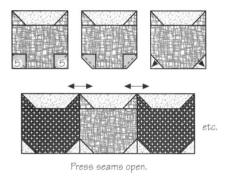

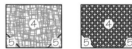

Press seams open.

8. Speed-piece a background 5 to the bottom corners of 1 medium 4 and 1 dark 4 for the bottom corner blocks.

9. Speed-piece medium or dark ear piece 5 to the bottom corners of the remaining piece 4. Add medium squares to dark heads and dark squares to medium heads. Make 19 dark heads and 19 medium heads. Sew the heads into 2 vertical strips of 19 heads each, alternating dark and medium heads. Begin one strip with a dark head and the other strip with a medium head.

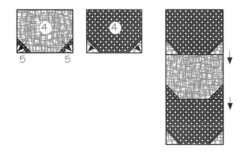

10. Add top corner blocks to the top of each vertical strip and the bottom corner blocks to the bottom of each vertical strip.

11. Sew the pieced strips to the top and bottom edges first, then to the sides of the quilt top. Press seam allowances toward inner border.

12. Sew the outer border to the top and bottom edges first, then to the sides of the quilt top. Press seam allowances toward the outer border.

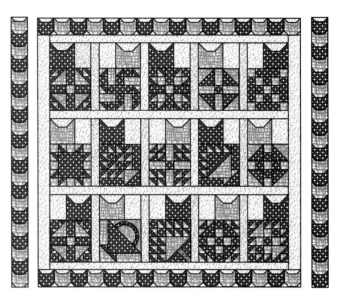

13. Layer the quilt top with batting and backing; baste.

14. Quilt each cat in lines radiating from either the bottom right or bottom left corner. Quilt straight lines down the center of the sashing strips and inner borders. Quilt whiskers on every second or third cat in the border.

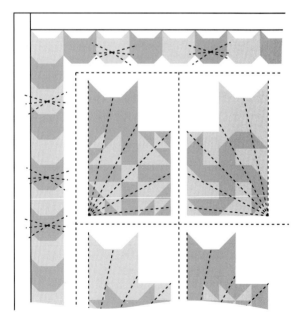

15. Bind the edges of the quilt.

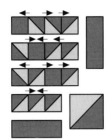

SAMPLER BLOCKS

Pine Tree

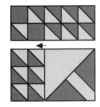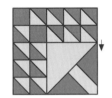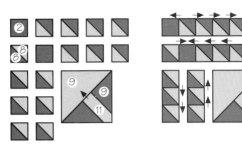

Fabric	Piece No.	No. of Pieces	Dimension
Medium	8	7	1⅞" x 1⅞"*
	9	1	3⅞" x 3⅞"*
	11	1	1½" x 2¾"
Dark	2	2	1½" x 1½"
	8	7	1⅞" x 1⅞"*
	9	1	3⅞" x 3⅞"*

You will use only 1 half-square unit from pieces 9; use extra for Cake Stand if desired.

Grape Basket

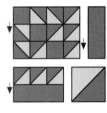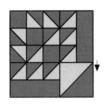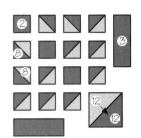

Fabric	Piece No.	No. of Pieces	Dimension
Medium	8	6	1⅞" x 1⅞"*
	12	1	2⅞" x 2⅞"*
Dark	2	3	1½" x 1½"
	3	2	1½" x 3½"
	8	6	1⅞" x 1⅞"*
	12	1	2⅞" x 2⅞"*

You will use only 1 half-square unit from piece 12.

Duck and Ducklings

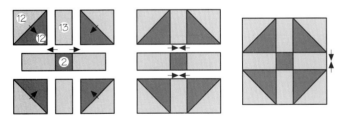

Fabric	Piece No.	No. of Pieces	Dimension
Medium	12	2	2⅞" x 2⅞"*
	13	4	1½" x 2½"
Dark	2	1	1½" x 1½"
	12	2	2⅞" x 2⅞"*

Basket

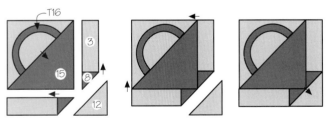

Fabric	Piece No.	No. of Pieces	Dimension
Medium	3	2	1½" x 3½"
	12	1	2⅞" x 2⅞" ◻
	15	1	4⅞" x 4⅞"*
Dark	8	1	1⅞" x 1⅞" ◻
	15	1	4⅞" x 4⅞"*
	T16	1	on page 85

You will use only 1 half-square unit from piece 15.

*See page 9 for speed-piecing half-square units.

Birds in Flight

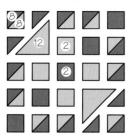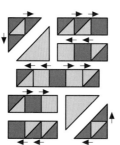

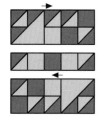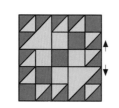

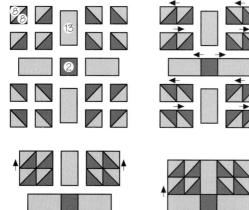

Fabric	Piece No.	No. of Pieces	Dimension
Medium	2	4	1½" x 1½"
	8	5	1⅞" x 1⅞"*
	12	1	2⅞" x 2⅞" ◻
Dark	2	5	1½" x 1½"
	8	7	1⅞" x 1⅞"*
			(speed-piece only 5 of 7)
			Cut 2 ◻

Aunt Kate's Choice

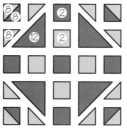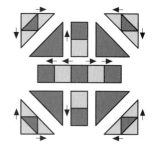

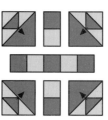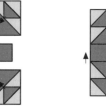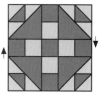

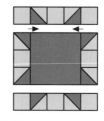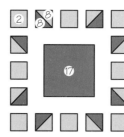

Fabric	Piece No.	No. of Pieces	Dimension
Medium	2	4	1½" x 1½"
	8	6	1⅞" x 1⅞"*
			(speed-piece only 2 of 6)
			Cut 4 ◻
Dark	2	5	1½" x 1½"
	8	2	1⅞" x 1⅞"*
	12	2	2⅞" x 2⅞" ◻

Handy Andy

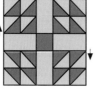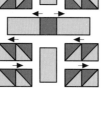

Fabric	Piece No.	No. of Pieces	Dimension
Medium	8	8	1⅞" x 1⅞"*
	13	4	1½" x 2½"
Dark	2	1	1½" x 1½"
	8	8	1⅞" x 1⅞"*

Farmer's Daughter

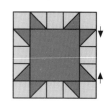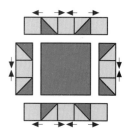

Fabric	Piece No.	No. of Pieces	Dimension
Medium	2	8	1½" x 1½"
	8	4	1⅞" x 1⅞"*
Dark	8	4	1⅞" x 1⅞"*
	17	1	3½" x 3½"

 *See page 9 for speed-piecing half-square units.

Cross and Crown

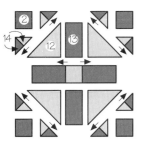
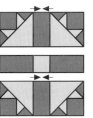
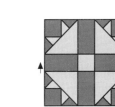

Fabric	Piece No.	No. of Pieces	Dimension
Medium	2	1	1½" x 1½"
	12	2	2⅞" x 2⅞" ◻
	14	2	2¼" x 2¼" ⊠
Dark	2	4	1½" x 1½"
	13	4	1½" x 2½"
	14	2	2¼" x 2¼" ⊠

Whirligig

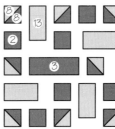
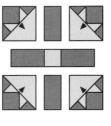
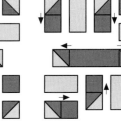
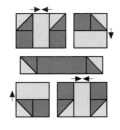
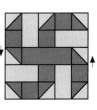
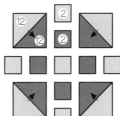
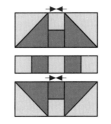

Fabric	Piece No.	No. of Pieces	Dimension
Medium	8	4	1⅞" x 1⅞"*
	13	4	1½" x 2½"
Dark	2	6	1½" x 1½"
	3	1	1½" x 3½"
	8	4	1⅞" x 1⅞"*

Country Lanes

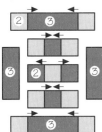
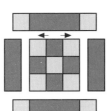
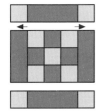

Fabric	Piece No.	No. of Pieces	Dimension
Medium	2	9	1½" x 1½"
Dark	2	4	1½" x 1½"
	3	4	1½" x 3½"

*See page 9 for speed-piecing half-square units.

Double Wrench

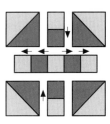
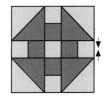
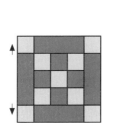

Fabric	Piece No.	No. of Pieces	Dimension
Medium	2	5	1½" x 1½"
	12	2	2⅞" x 2⅞"*
Dark	2	4	1½" x 1½"
	12	2	2⅞" x 2⅞"*

Fox and Geese

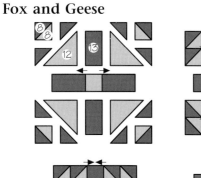

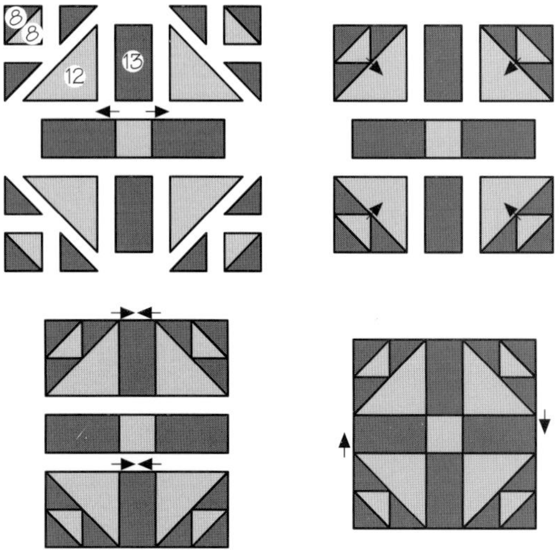

Fabric	Piece No.	No. of Pieces	Dimension
Medium	2	1	1½" x 1½"
	8	2	1⅞" x 1⅞"*
	12	2	2⅞" x 2⅞" ◹
Dark	8	6	1⅞" x 1⅞"*
			(speed-piece only 2 of 6)
			Cut 4 ◹
	13	4	1½" x 2½"

Sister's Choice

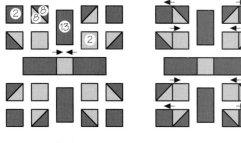

Fabric	Piece No.	No. of Pieces	Dimension
Medium	2	5	1½" x 1½"
	8	4	1⅞" x 1⅞"*
Dark	2	4	1½" x 1½"
	8	4	1⅞" x 1⅞"*
	13	4	1½" x 2½"

Cake Stand

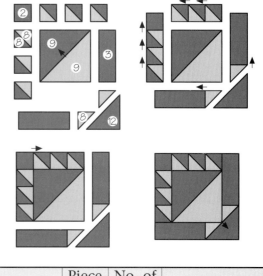

Fabric	Piece No.	No. of Pieces	Dimension
Medium	8	4	1⅞" x 1⅞"*
			(speed-piece only 3 of 4)
			Cut 1 ◹
	9	1	3⅞" x 3⅞"*
Dark	2	1	1½" x 1½"
	3	2	1½" x 3½"
	8	3	1⅞" x 1⅞"*
	9	1	3⅞" x 3⅞"*
	12	1	2⅞" x 2⅞" ◹

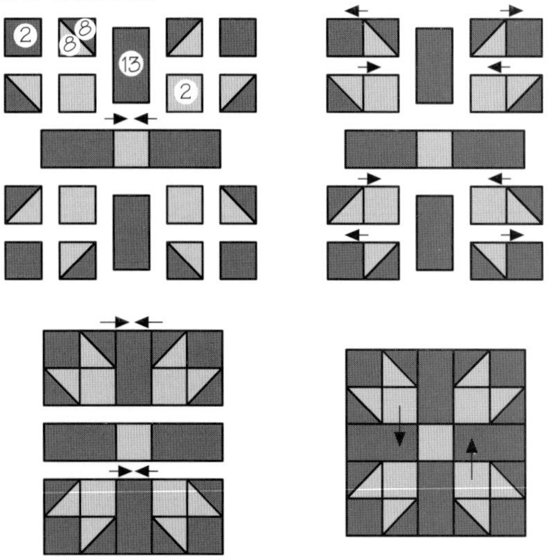

You will use only 1 half-square unit from pieces 9; use extra for Pine Trees if desired.

ALPHABET AND NUMBER BLOCKS

You can substitute letters of the alphabet or numbers for the pieced sampler blocks to spell out a name, date, or a phrase. See "Noel" on page 29 for one very simple, but delightful example.

Cut the required number of pieces for each block, using the dimensions in the chart below:

1	1½" x 1½"	7	2½" x 3½"
2	1½" x 2½"	8	2½" x 4½"
3	1½" x 3½"	9	3½" x 3½"
4	1½" x 4½"	10	3½" x 4½"
5	1½" x 5½"	11	4½" x 4½"
6	2½" x 2½"		

Assemble the pieces, following the piecing diagrams on page 81. Press all seam allowances toward the darker fabric.

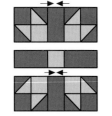

See page 9 for speed-piecing half-square units.

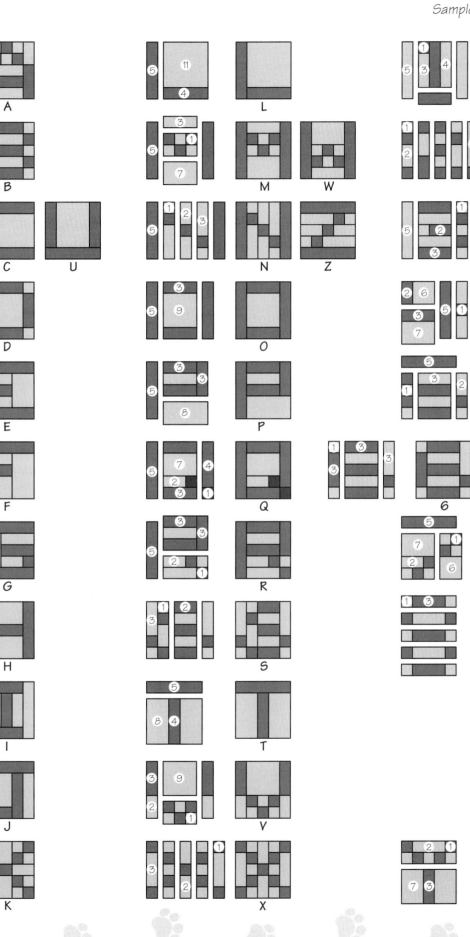

A

B

C U

D

E

F

G

H

I

J

K

L

M W

N Z

O

P

Q

R

S

T

V

X

1

2

3

4

5

6 9

7

8

Y

Kelvie's Kitties

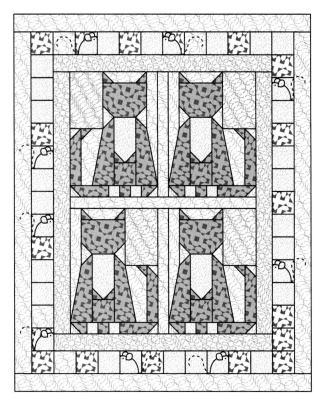

This cat, with his contrasting bib and feet, is a slightly more challenging pieced block than most in this book. Although rotary cutting and speed piecing can be employed at most steps, a few pieces require templates and there are some inset seams. The little Drunkard's Path mice in the border are only 1½" square—not much bigger than the real thing!

Color photo:	page 24
Quilt Size:	21" x 25½"
Finished Block Size:	6" x 8¼"

MATERIALS: 44"-wide fabric

¼ yd. for cats
⅛ yd. OR scraps for dickey and paws
¼ yd. total of scraps for pieced border
Scraps for mice
¾ yd. for background, sashing, inner and outer borders, and binding
¾ yd. for backing
Embroidery floss for mouse details

CUTTING

Use templates on pages 85–86.

Note: The squares and rectangles you cut may not look like the corresponding pieces in the block diagram because some of the diagonals are speed-pieced. The diagram shows you the location of each piece, not necessarily its actual shape.

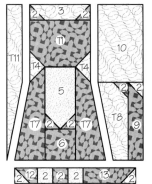

	Piece No.	No. of Pieces	Dimension
Cat Fabric			
Cats	T1	4	
	2	24	1¼" x 1¼"
	6	4	2" x 2"
	T7	4 and 4r	
	9	4	1¼" x 4¼"
	12	4	1¼" x 1⅝"
	13	4	1¼" x 3⅛"
Dickey Fabric			
Dickey	2	8	1¼" x 1¼"
	5	4	2" x 3½"
Pieced Border Fabrics			
		50	2" x 2"
Mouse Fabric			
Mouse	T14	9	
	T15	9	
	T16	9	
Background Fabric			
Cats	2	12	1¼" x 1¼"
	3	4	1¼" x 3½"
	T4	4 and 4r	
	T8	3 and 1r	
	10	4	2¾" x 4¼"
	T11	3 and 1r	

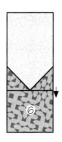

	No. of Pieces	Dimension
Background Fabric		
Vertical sashing strips	2	1¼" x 8¾"
Horizontal sashing strips	1	1¼" x 13¼"
Inner border sides	2	1⅝" x 17¾"
Inner border top & bottom	1	1½" x 15½"
	1	1¾" x 15½"
Outer border sides	2	1¾" x 23"
Outer border top & bottom	2	1¾" x 21"

PIECING THE BLOCKS

Press all seam allowances in the direction of the arrows unless otherwise instructed.

1. To make the ear unit, speed-piece a cat 2 to each end of a background 3.

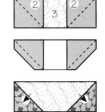

2. To make the head unit, sew a background 4 to the bottom corners of a cat 1, stopping and backstitching ¼" from the inner edge as shown. Trim off the points.

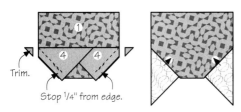

3. Sew ear unit to head unit.

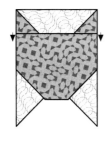

4. To make the dickey unit, speed-piece a cat 2 to the bottom corners of a dickey 5. Sew one side, trim, and press; then sew the other side.

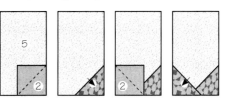

5. Sew a cat 6 to the bottom of the dickey unit.

6. Sew a cat 7 to each side of the dickey unit, matching the top and bottom edges.

7. Sew the head unit to the body unit. This is an inset seam and is a little more difficult than a simple straight seam. Do not try to sew the head to the body in one long seam. Instead sew 3 separate seams from dot to dot on Templates 1, 4, and 7. Pin at the dots on Templates 4 and 7 and sew only from pin to pin, backstitching at each end for strength. Push all seam allowances out of the way so you don't catch them in the seam. After each seam, remove the piece from the sewing machine and snip threads. Pin the next seam at the dots on Template 1 and sew the seam from pin to pin, backstitching at each end. Then sew the third seam from dot to dot on Templates 4 and 7.

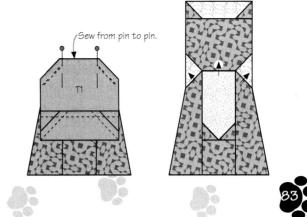

8. To make the tail unit, speed-piece a cat 2 to a background 8; speed-piece a background 2 to a cat 9. Sew each pair of units together. Make 3 as shown for right-tailed cats; reverse the speed-pieced angles for the left-tailed cat.

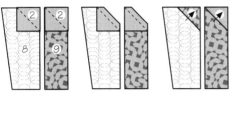

Right-tailed cats
Make 3.

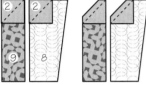

Left-tailed cat
Make 1.

9. Sew a background 10 to the top of each tail unit. On the inner edge only, sew to the dot on Template 8; backstitch.

Sew only to dot and backstitch.

10. Sew the side unit and a background 11 to the head/body unit; make 3 as shown and 1 reversed. Sew each side in 2 steps: Stitch from the top and bottom edges to the dot on Template 11 and on Template 8; backstitch at the dots to secure the seams. Press seam allowances toward the side sections.

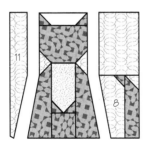

11. To make the foot unit for the right-tailed cat, speed-piece a background 2 to the left side of a cat 12, and a background 2 to the right side of a cat 13. To make foot unit for left-tailed cat, speed-piece a background 2 to the right side of a cat 12, and a background 2 to the left side of a cat 13.

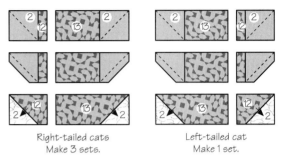

Right-tailed cats
Make 3 sets.

Left-tailed cat
Make 1 set.

12. To complete the foot unit, sew the units made in step 11, 2 dickey 2 pieces and a cat 2 piece as shown.

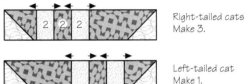

Right-tailed cats
Make 3.

Left-tailed cat
Make 1.

13. Sew the foot unit to the body unit. Press seam allowances toward the feet.

ASSEMBLING AND FINISHING THE QUILT TOP

1. Sew the Cat blocks together into 2 rows of 2 each, with vertical sashing strips between the blocks.
2. Sew the horizontal sashing strip between the top and bottom rows. Press seam allowances toward the sashing strip.

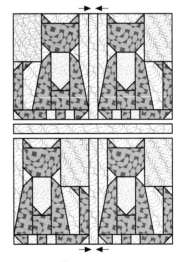

3. Sew the inner border to the sides first, then to the top and bottom edges of the quilt top. Press seam allowances toward the inner border.

4. For each of the 9 Mouse blocks, use the paper-patch method on pages 9–10 to prepare 9 each of T14, T15, and T16. Turn under only the curved edge of T14. Appliqué the curved edge of each mouse body to a border square, tucking 1 ear underneath and appliquéing 1 ear on top. Make 5 mice face right and 4 face left.

5. Arrange the border squares and mouse squares around the quilt, 10 each for the top and bottom borders and 15 each for the side borders. Sew the squares together for each

6. border and press all seam allowances in one direction.

7. Sew the pieced strips to the top and bottom edges of the quilt top first, then to the sides. Press seam allowances toward the inner border.

8. Sew the outer border to the top and bottom edges first, then to the sides of the quilt top. Press seam allowances toward the outer border.

9. Layer the quilt top with batting and backing; baste.

10. Quilt around the cats, dickeys, feet, and mice. Quilt or embroider the mouse tails in contrasting thread. Embroider mouse eyes, nose, and whiskers.

11. Bind the edges of the quilt.

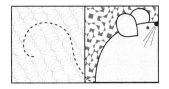

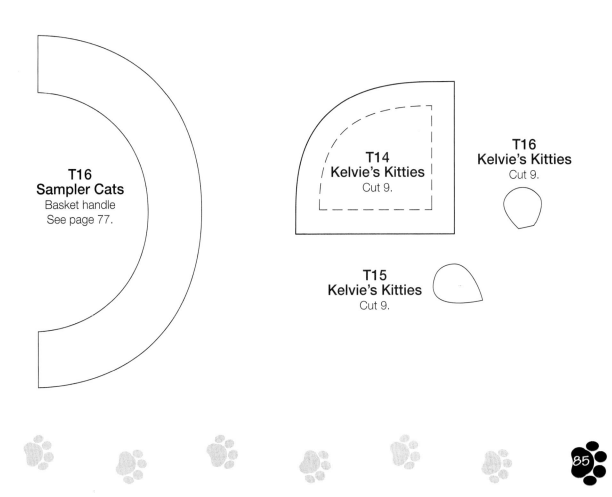

T16
Sampler Cats
Basket handle
See page 77.

T14
Kelvie's Kitties
Cut 9.

T16
Kelvie's Kitties
Cut 9.

T15
Kelvie's Kitties
Cut 9.

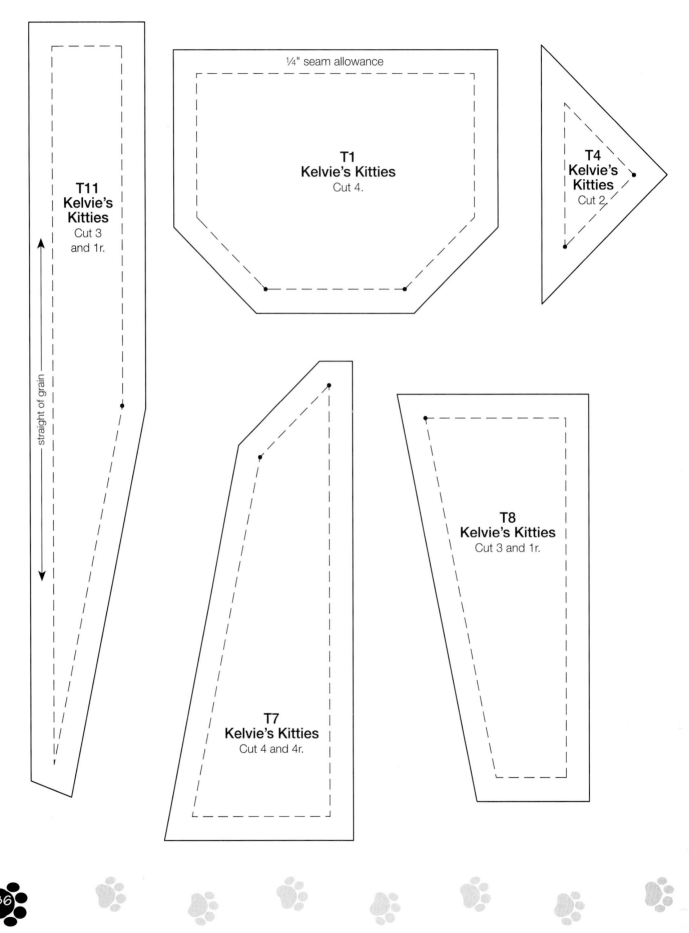

¼" seam allowance

T1
Kelvie's Kitties
Cut 4.

T4
Kelvie's Kitties
Cut 2.

T11
Kelvie's Kitties
Cut 3 and 1r.

straight of grain

T7
Kelvie's Kitties
Cut 4 and 4r.

T8
Kelvie's Kitties
Cut 3 and 1r.

Fish Dreams

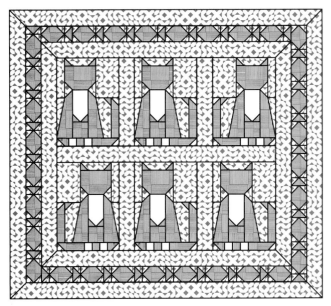

The little speed-pieced fish take some time to sew, but they make a charming border. If they are made from similar fabrics, they tend to run together, so at first the viewer might not notice that they are fish. I like to put little surprises like this in my quilts. If you would like the fish more visible, make each one different from the fish next to it—alternate two fabrics or make the fish in a variety of colors.

Color photograph: page 25
Quilt Size: 32½" x 29½"
Finished Block Size: Cats 6" x 8¼"
Fish 1½" x 3"

MATERIALS: 44"-wide fabric

⅓ yd. total OR scraps of 6 fabrics for cats
⅛ yd. total OR scraps for dickey and paws
¼ yd. total OR scraps for fish
1½ yds. for background, sashing, borders, and binding
1 yd. for backing

CUTTING

Use templates on page 86.

Note: The squares and rectangles you cut may not look like the corresponding pieces in the block diagram because some of the diagonals are

speed-pieced. The diagram shows you the location of each piece, not necessarily its actual shape.

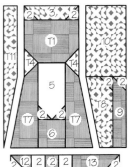
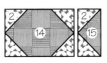

	Piece No.	No. of Pieces	Dimension
From each of 6 fabrics for cats, cut:			
Cats	T1	1	
	2	6	1¼" x 1¼"
	6	1	2" x 2"
	T7	1 and 1r	
	9	1	1¼" x 4¼"
	12	1	1¼" x 1⅝"
	13	1	1¼" x 3⅛"
Dickey Fabric			
Dickeys	2	12	1¼" x 1¼"
	5	6	2" x 3½"
Fish Fabric			
Fish	14	32	2" x 2¾"
	15	32	1¼" x 2"
Background Fabric			
Cats	2	18	1¼" x 1¼"
	3	6	1¼" x 3½"
	T4	3	2¾" x 2¾" Cut squares ⊠
	T8	4 and 2r	
	10	6	2¾" x 4¼"
	T11	4 and 2r	
Fish	2	192	1¼" x 1¼"
Vertical sashing strips		4	2" x 8¾"
Horizontal sashing strips		1	2" x 21½"
Inner border sides		2	2" x 23"
Inner border top & bottom		2	2" x 26"
Outer border sides		2	3" x 32"
Outer border top & bottom		2	3" x 35"

PIECING THE BLOCKS

Follow instructions for Kelvie's Kitties on pages 83–84 to make 4 cats with tails on the right and 2 cats with tails on the left.

ASSEMBLING THE QUILT TOP

1. Sew the Cat blocks into 2 rows of 3 blocks each, with vertical sashing strips between the blocks.
2. Sew the horizontal sashing strip between the top and bottom rows. Press seam allowances toward the sashing strip.

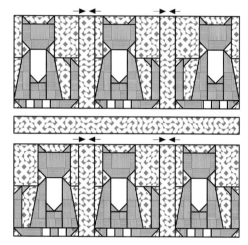

3. Sew the inner border to the quilt top, following directions on page 11 for borders with mitered corners. Press seam allowances toward the inner border.

FISH BLOCK BORDER

1. To make the fish body, speed-piece a background 2 to each corner of a fish 14. Sew, trim, and press the corners on one side first, then sew the remaining corners.

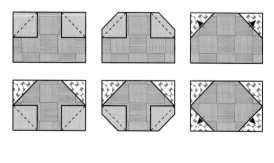

2. To make the fish tail, speed-piece a background 2 to the upper left and lower left corners of a fish 15 as shown.

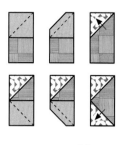

3. Sew the tail unit to the body unit. Press seam allowances open to reduce bulk.

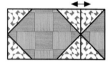

4. Sew 8 fish together, facing in the same direction, end-to-end for each of the top, bottom, and side border strips.

5. Sew the top and bottom pieced borders to the quilt first, paying careful attention to the direction the fish are swimming. The fish appear to be moving in one continuous circle around the quilt. Then, sew the side pieced borders to the quilt top. Press seam allowances toward the inner border.

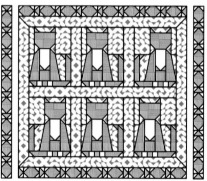

FINISHING

1. Sew the outer border to the quilt top, following directions on page 11 for borders with mitered corners. Press seam allowances toward the outer border.
2. Layer the quilt top with batting and backing; baste.
3. Quilt around each cat, dickey, cat foot, and fish.
4. Bind the edges of the quilt.

Puss in the Center

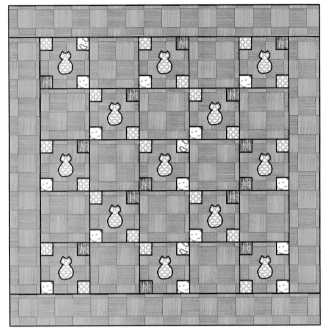

This is the traditional Puss in the Corner block with printed cats appliquéd in the 3" center squares. You could feature any other printed animal in the center squares: teddy bears, sheep, dogs, cows, bunnies—there are so many choices these days. Combine many different animals and make a farm quilt or a jungle quilt. If you really enjoy searching for just the right fabrics, find an animal for each letter of the alphabet and make an alphabet quilt.

This is a rotary-cut, Template-Free®, speed-pieced design. It is simple enough to be your first rotary-cutting project.

Color photo:	page 21
Quilt Size:	38½" x 38½"
Finished Block Size:	6" x 6"

MATERIALS

½–1 yd. cat print (enough to cut 13 motifs 3½" x 3½")
2 yds. for background, border, and binding
⅛ yd. each of 10 solids
1¼ yds. for backing

CUTTING

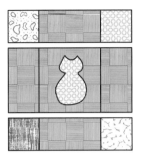

1. From template plastic, cut a 3½" x 3½" square. Center the plastic square over the cat print and cut out 13 cats. If it is not possible to isolate individual cats in a 3" x 3" finished square, cut around each cat motif, adding ⅛" to turn under.
2. From background fabric, first cut borders from the lengthwise grain of the fabric before cutting block pieces.
   - 2 strips, each 4½" x 30½", for side borders
   - 2 strips, each 4½" x 38½", for top and bottom borders

   Cut additional pieces from remaining background fabric:
   - 13 squares, each 3½" x 3½" (These are needed only if you cut out and appliqué individual cats.)
   - 26 rectangles, each 2" x 3½"
   - 5 strips, each 3½" x 13"
   - 12 squares, each 6½" x 6½"
3. From each of the 10 solids, cut:
   - 1 strip, 2" x 13", for a total of 10 strips

PIECING THE BLOCKS

Press all seam allowances in the direction of the arrows unless otherwise instructed.

1. If you are going to appliqué the cats, center each on a 3½" square of background fabric and pin. Appliqué in place, turning under ⅛" as you stitch. (See pages 9–10 for Paper-Patch Appliqué.)
2. Sew a 2" x 3½" background rectangle to the left and right sides of the cat squares.

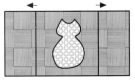

3. Sew a different color 2" x 13" strip on each side of a 3½" x 13" background strip to make 5 strip units. From the strip units, cut a total of 26 segments, each 2" wide.

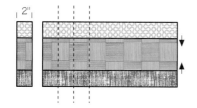

4. Sew the segments to the top and bottom of each cat square, randomly placing the solid colors.

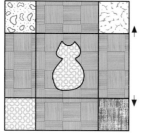

ASSEMBLING AND FINISHING THE QUILT TOP

1. Arrange the Cat blocks and 6½" background squares into 5 rows of 5 blocks each, alternating plain squares and blocks as shown below. Sew the blocks together in horizontal rows. Press seam allowances toward the plain squares.

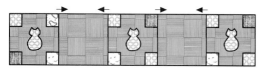

2. Sew the rows together. Press seam allowances in one direction.
3. Sew the borders to the sides first, then to the top and bottom edges of the quilt top. Press seam allowances toward the borders.
4. Layer the quilt top with batting and backing; baste.
5. Quilt around each cat motif. Quilt in straight lines that just touch the outside corners of the colored squares, but do not quilt through the cat motifs. In each 6½" background square, quilt a large cat paw. Quilt small cat paws, traveling in one direction all around the border; place each paw 1"–3" from the previous one.

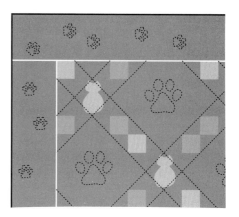

6. Bind the edges of the quilt.

Cowboy Cats

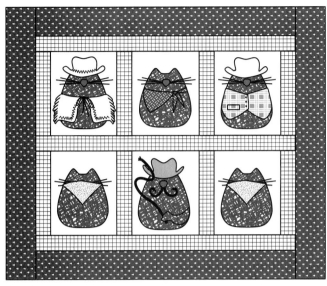

All sorts of fabrics and embellishments add to the fun of this quilt. If you enjoy driving all over town to find just the right star for a sheriff's badge, this is the quilt for you.

Color photo: page 28
Quilt Size: 43½" x 36½"
Finished Block Size: 9" x 11"

MATERIALS: 44"-wide fabric

¼ yd. each of 5 fabrics for cats
¾ yd. for background
Scraps of western-print fabric for cactus cut-outs (optional)
Scraps of Ultrasuede™ or felt
⅝ yd. for sashing
1¼ yds. for border and binding
1½ yds. for backing
2 yds. gold yarn or ⅛"-wide leather strips
Scraps for bandannas and sheriff's vest
3 buttons, ¼" diameter
1" brass watch charm
1½" brass star charm
3 packages of whiskers or paint-brush bristles for stuffed animals
Scraps of iron-on fusible web
White glue

CUTTING

Use templates on pages 94–96.

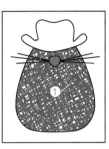

	Piece No.	No. of Pieces	Dimension
Cat Fabrics			
Bodies	1	6	
Tail	10	1	
		(to match bad-guy cat)	
Background Fabric			
Blocks		6	9½" x 11½"
Ultrasuede or Felt			
Good-guy hats	2	2	
Bad-guy hat	9	1	
Noses	3	4	
Chaps	4	1 and 1r	
Scraps			
Good-guy bandanna	5	1	
Good-guy bandanna	6	1	
Bandanna tie	7	2	
Sheriff's vest	8	1 and 1r	
Vest pocket		1	1½" x 2"
Bad-guy bandanna		2	4½" x 4½"
Sashing Fabric			
Vertical strips		8	2½" x 11½"
Horizontal strips		3	2½" x 35½"
Border Fabric			
Sides		2	4½" x 36½"
Top and bottom		2	4½" x 35½"

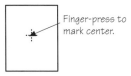

APPLIQUÉING THE BLOCKS

Use the paper-patch method on pages 9–10 to prepare appliqué pieces as indicated.

1. Fold background block in half once, then in half again, and finger-press the crease to mark the center.

Finger-press to mark center.

2. Paper-patch 6 cat bodies. Pin the paper-patched cats to the background blocks, matching the center dot on the cat template to the center crease on the block.

3. Select cactus motifs. Following manufacturer's directions, fuse webbing to wrong side of fabric. Cut out motifs. To adhere motifs to blocks, peel off paper and arrange motifs around the cats. Following manufacturer's directions, press in place. Fuse some motifs behind cats before appliquéing the cat bodies, and some motifs on top of cats after appliquéing the cat bodies.

4. Appliqué cat bodies in place.

5. *Cowboy with chaps:* Position the hat and appliqué. (It isn't necessary to turn under the edge of Ultrasuede or felt.) If desired, use a decorative machine stitch to add a hatband. Use a decorative machine stitch to sew the chaps in place. Cut fringe as indicated on Template T4, clipping about 1" deep and 1/8" apart. Cut 1 strip of Ultrasuede 1/8" x 12" and tie a bow; tack to the center of the chaps.

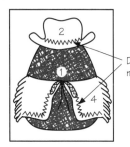

Decorative machine stitching

6. *Cowboy with bandanna:* Paper-patch bandanna pieces 5 and 6 and appliqué to the cat. With right sides together, sew bandanna tie (Template 7), leaving a 1" opening for turning. Turn inside out and close opening with

a blind stitch. Make a knot in the tie and tack where bandanna pieces 5 and 6 meet.

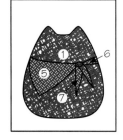

Leave opening.

7. *Sheriff:* Appliqué Ultrasuede hat (Template 2).Paper-patch both vest pieces (Template 8 and 8r) and appliqué to the cat. Fold the vest pocket piece in half lengthwise, wrong sides together. Sew each end with a 1/8"-wide seam. Turn inside out and press under 1/4" on the raw edges. With the folded edge on top, appliqué only the bottom and sides of the pocket to the vest, leaving folded edge free.

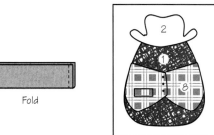

Fold

Sew 3 buttons down the center of the sheriff's vest. Add a watch charm above the pocket so it appears partially tucked inside the pocket. Add a star charm to the opposite side of the vest.

8. *Bandits:* Fold the bandanna squares in half diagonally, right sides together. Sew along both raw edges, leaving a 1" opening for turning. Turn inside out and close opening with a blind stitch. Roll up a 1" diameter ball of batting; tack securely to the cat to make a nose that will push out the bandanna. Appliqué the top edge of the bandanna and about 1" down each side to cover the nose.

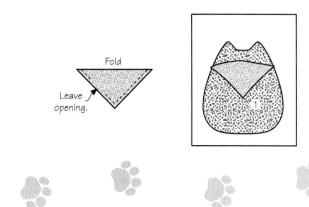

Fold

Leave opening.

9. *Bad guy:* Appliqué Ultrasuede hat (Template 9). Braid a 12" whip from 3 strands of yarn or 3 strands of ⅛"-wide leather strips. Wrap bottom 4" of whip with contrasting leather or yarn. Paper-patch the tail (Template 10) and press. Appliqué the tail in place, with the end of the tail covering a portion of the whip handle. Leave a small portion free to remove the paper, then finish the tail.

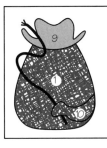

ASSEMBLING AND FINISHING THE QUILT TOP

1. Arrange the Cat blocks in 2 rows of 3 blocks each. Sew blocks in horizontal rows, with vertical sashing strips between the blocks and at each end of a row.

2. Sew a horizontal sashing strip between the rows and to the top and bottom edges of the quilt top. Press seam allowances toward the sashing strips.

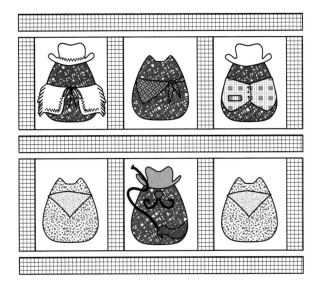

3. Sew borders to the top and bottom edges first, then to the sides of the quilt top. Press seam allowances toward the border.

4. Layer the quilt top with batting and backing; baste.

5. Quilt around each cat, around each block, and between sashing strips and outer border.

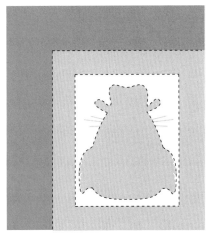

6. Adding noses and whiskers: Cut paint-brush bristles 2" long (3" long for bad guy), or if using packaged animal whiskers fused at one end, divide each set where fused into 2 sets of whiskers. Iron a scrap of fusible web to 4 squares of scrap fabric, each about ½" x ½". Refer to Template 1 for the position of the nose and whiskers. Position whiskers, peel paper from fused square of fabric, and press over the center of whiskers to hold them in place. (Before you do this, test the iron's heat by pressing one of the whiskers onto a piece of scrap fabric, to be sure the whiskers won't melt. If they do, attach whiskers with white glue.) Appliqué noses (Template 3) over whiskers. Curl bad-guy whiskers into a mustache and couch in place with matching or nylon thread. For bandits, tuck a few whiskers under the top edge of the bandanna and glue in place.

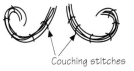

Couching stitches

7. Bind the edges of the quilt.

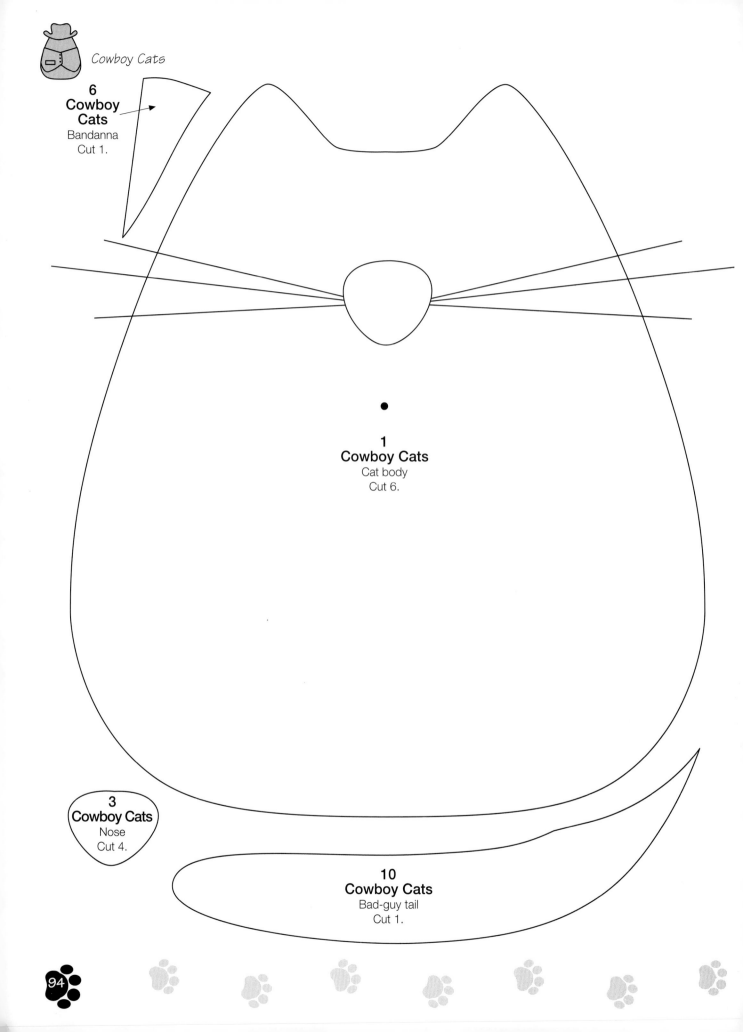

6
Cowboy Cats
Bandanna
Cut 1.

1
Cowboy Cats
Cat body
Cut 6.

3
Cowboy Cats
Nose
Cut 4.

10
Cowboy Cats
Bad-guy tail
Cut 1.

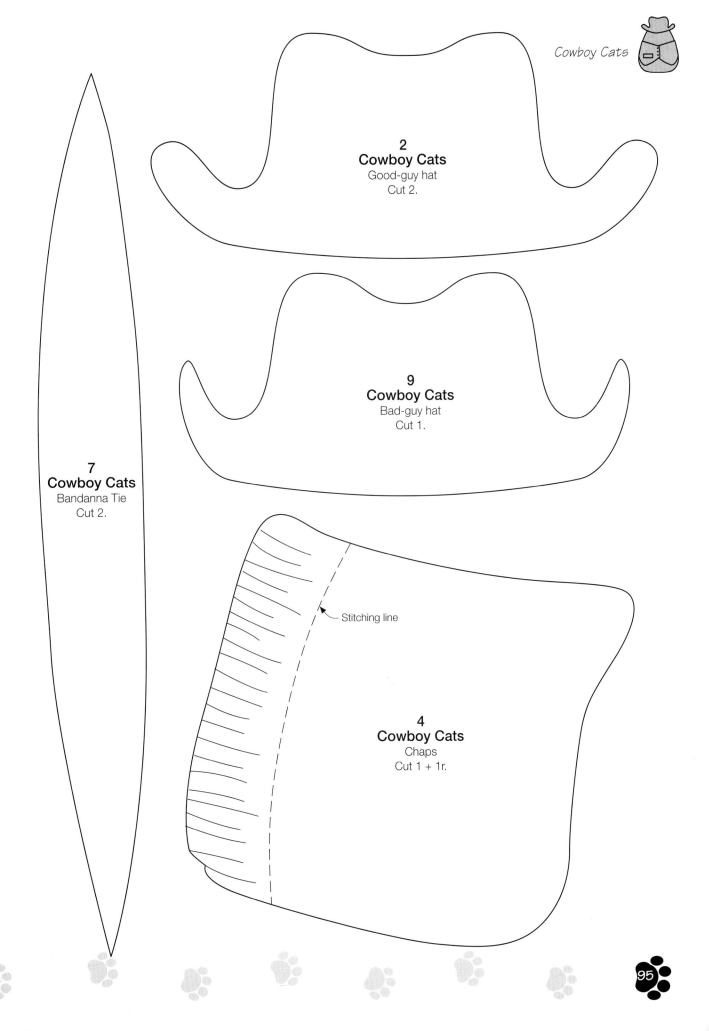

2
Cowboy Cats
Good-guy hat
Cut 2.

9
Cowboy Cats
Bad-guy hat
Cut 1.

7
Cowboy Cats
Bandanna Tie
Cut 2.

Stitching line

4
Cowboy Cats
Chaps
Cut 1 + 1r.

Cowboy Cats

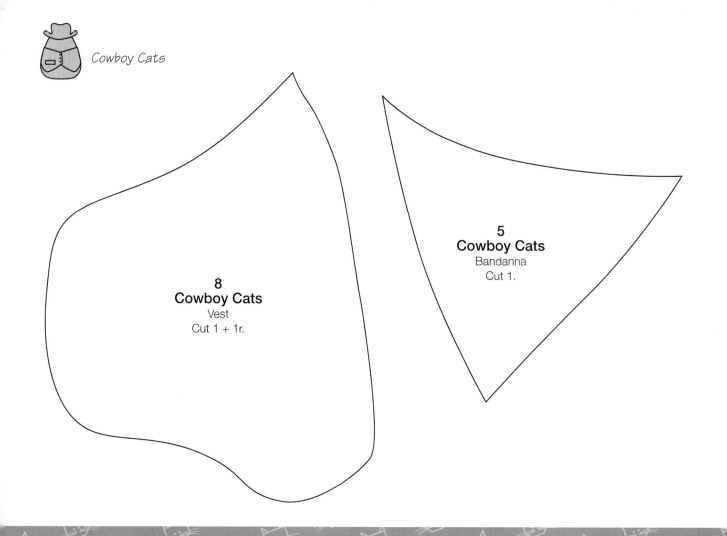

8
Cowboy Cats
Vest
Cut 1 + 1r.

5
Cowboy Cats
Bandanna
Cut 1.

MEET THE AUTHOR

Janet Kime teaches and lectures about quiltmaking throughout the Pacific Northwest, curates a quilt show at an arts center each summer, and writes the newsletter for her local quilt guild, Needle and I. In addition to her busy schedule of quilting activities, Janet is an academic counselor at the University of Washington in Seattle. She and her two goats live on rural Vashon Island, where several cats allow her to share their home.